# G. RAYMOND CARLSON

# OUR FAITH

## AND

# FELLOWSHIP

Radiant BOOKS

Gospel Publishing House/Springfield. Mo. 65802

02-0908

OUR FAITH AND FELLOWSHIP
©1977 by the Gospel Publishing House
Springfield, Missouri 65802. All rights reserved.
Adapted from the Christian Faith Series manual *Our Faith and Fellowship* by Ralph W. Harris, © 1963 by the Gospel Publishing House.
Library of Congress Catalog Card Number 77-075023
International Standard Book Number 0-88243-908-1
Printed in the United States of America


Teacher's guide for individual or group study with this book is available from the Gospel Publishing House (order number 32-0178).

# *Foreword*

The 20th century has seen a remarkable revival—a Pentecostal revival. From flickering flames scattered here and there at the turn of the century, the revival has spread like a mighty forest fire until today millions have been affected. Since mid-century, vast numbers of people in the old-line denominations have received the baptism in the Holy Spirit with the evidence of speaking in other tongues.

The Assemblies of God, organized in 1914, is the largest of the Pentecostal groups. Assemblies of God adherents worldwide total nearly 6 million.

The purpose of this book is to present a declaration of the beliefs of the Assemblies of God, as contained in its Statement of Fundamental Truths. The preamble of the Statement declares:

> The Bible is our all-sufficient rule for faith and practice. This Statement of Fundamental Truths is intended simply as a basis of fellowship among us (i.e., that we all speak the same thing, 1 Cor. 1:10; Acts 2:42). The phraseology employed in this Statement is not inspired or contended for, but the truth set forth is held to be essential to a full-gospel ministry. No claim is made that it contains all Biblical truth, only that it covers our need as to these fundamental doctrines.

The full Statement of Fundamental Truths will be found on page 124.

May you find this study of the basic beliefs of the Assemblies of God interesting and beneficial.

# *Contents*

# 1
## *The Bible Is God's Word*

*Read:* Luke 24:27; John 5:39, 46; 2 Timothy 2:15; 3:14-17; 1 Peter 1:10-12; 2 Peter 1:19-21. *Key Verse:* "Heaven and earth shall pass away, but my words shall not pass away" (Matthew 24:35). (See statement #1 on p. 124.)

The story is told of a little girl who wanted to give her father a Bible as a gift. She was very anxious to put an appropriate inscription on the flyleaf. Since her father was an author, he received many complimentary copies of the writings of others. Why not go to his library and look at the books he had received? Shortly she found what she wanted and carefully copied it. When her father opened the Bible he read: "To my darling daddy—with the compliments of the author."

The girl's motive was unexcelled. The inscription was penned with love. But her understanding of authorship was faulty.

The authorship of the Bible is vitally important. The Statement of Fundamental Truths declares it to be "our all-sufficient rule for faith and practice." Is it "verbally inspired of God"? Is it the "revelation of God to man"? Is it the "infallible, authoritative rule of faith and conduct"? Let's find the answers.

### Four Views of Scripture

Basically there are four main views of Scripture:
1. *The Bible is the work of man.* This is the posi-

5

tion of the atheists. People who have some sort of belief in God—rationalists, such as the old-line liberals—also ascribe the authorship of Scripture to man.

2. *The Bible contains the Word of God.* This view holds that the Bible is the Word of God in matters of faith and practice, but in other areas it is entirely human.

3. *The Bible becomes the Word of God.* This is the neoorthodox view. Despite giving lip service to Biblical terms, these proponents believe the Bible becomes the Word of God when a person experiences God in the reading of it. Truth must be experiential to them; it can have no objective, historic meaning.

4. *The Bible is verbally inspired.* We accept and defend this simple assertion.

## Has God Spoken?

Theology properly begins with one simple yet overwhelming fundamental principle—*God is.* The first great question then is: "Has God spoken?"

If there is a God, it must follow as night follows day that He has spoken. A God who doesn't or can't communicate with His creatures is as worthless to us as no god at all. For you to believe there is a God but to believe He has no Word, is to make your Creator less than yourself.

Through the centuries Christians have accepted the fact that God has spoken. With united voice Christianity has answered: "Yes, God has spoken uniquely through His inspired Word, the Bible, and supremely in His incarnate Son, Jesus Christ."

We live in an age that flaunts authority. Certain influential schools of thought have turned the historic assertion, "God has spoken," into the doubting question, "Has God spoken?" Satan, the father of lies, was the first to ask the question. He put it to Eve in Eden—"Hath God said?" That insinuation of doubt became the thin edge of the wedge by which he brought about the awful separation between man and God.

Change "thus saith the Lord" to "it seems to me," and you'll reduce the Bible to little more than a good place to look for solutions along with Ann Landers and *Peanuts*. Evangelist Billy Graham's ringing assertion, "the Bible says," attests to the enduring grip of Scripture on needy human hearts.

## What Is Certain?

The only basis for certainty in human life and thought is found in the sublime truth that God has spoken. Take away this foundation and Christianity will crumble. If we aren't sure about the Bible, we'll be unsure about our origin and destiny, the future, the supernatural, and the divine.

Meddle with the inspiration of the Scriptures, and before long you'll tamper with the person of Christ. Christ, the living Word, and the Bible, the written Word, are entwined and fit like hand in glove. All that we know of Christ we owe to the Bible. If we are uncertain about the supernatural origin of the Bible, how can we be sure about the Christ it presents?

Long ago God spoke "bit by bit and in many different ways" (Hebrews 1:1, *Williams*). During the centuries God had spoken in dreams, visions, types, and symbols. But now He has spoken "by his Son." The New Testament is the inspired record of the revelation of God in Christ.

The Bible, like the message on the walls of Belshazzer's palace, was written with the fingers of a man's hand. But the message is divine, inspired, inerrant, and infallible.

## Put It This Way

The Bible is a divine-human book. "Just a minute," you say. "What does that mean?" The answer is in Christ.

Christ is the divine-human, living Word and the Bible is the divine-human, written Word. This is the twofold foundation of Christian faith.

What do we mean? Simply this: God caused His Son to be born of a woman. Becoming the Son of Man, Christ shared in the personality characteristics of His mother—physically and psychologically. He resembled her in physical characteristics and was influenced by the intellectual and social setting of the home. He was Mary's son as well as God's Son.

## That's the Way It Is With the Bible

God could have dropped the Scriptures from heaven in a neatly bound book, but He didn't do it that way. He chose to use human authors. The light of revelation flashed on the minds and hearts of men such as Moses, David, Isaiah, John, and Paul. They wrote on papyrus, parchment, sheepskin, and goatskin.

Light is broken down into a variety of rays when it shines through a prism. That's what took place as God's light of truth came through the prisms of human personality. The Holy Spirit used the personalities and styles of the 40 some writers to convey the total of divine revelation in the 66 books of the Bible. This is evident in the language used—both in vocabulary and style—and in the diversity of emphases and methods of approach. The bluntness of Amos, the farmhand, is as equally the Word of God as the refined writing of the scholarly Isaiah.

The Bible had a human origin in that it came from the hands of the men who wrote it. *But* its ultimate source was divine! The Holy Spirit inspired the men who wrote it. That makes it unique.

## Christ's Testimony

Christ accepted the Scriptures as the supreme testimony of the Father.

1. *He believed the Scriptures.* On the way to the Mount of Olives he turned to the disciples and said: "You will all fall away." He quoted Scripture, saying: "It is written . . . " (Mark 14:27, RSV), to support His assertion. Repeatedly He predicted His death and resurrection. (Read Luke 24:25-27; Matthew 5:18; John 10:35).

2. *He obeyed the Scriptures.* Even more impressive than the fact that Jesus believed the Scriptures is that He obeyed them. A striking example occurred during His temptation in the wilderness. He obeyed the written Word. It was as much the standard of His behavior as the criterion of His belief. (Compare Mark 8:31; 14:21; Luke 18:31; 24:26; John 9:4; Matthew 26:54.)

3. *He quoted the Scriptures.* With all His supernatural knowledge and wisdom, Jesus accepted and endorsed the divine origin and authority of the Old Testament. The Gospels are full of His quotations.

Why did Jesus attach such importance to the Scriptures? Isn't the revelation of God in nature sufficient? True, God has revealed himself in nature (Psalm 19:1-6). But such revelation did not lead man to God. Men became worshipers of nature instead of worshipers of God, changing "the glory of the uncorruptible God into an image made like to corruptible man, and to birds, and four-footed beasts, and creeping things" (Romans 1:23).

God has chosen to reveal himself through His eternal, written Word. It is this written Word which we now possess and handle that came through men as they were moved by the Holy Spirit (2 Peter 1:21). The Bible comes to us as the very Word of God, with all the truth, dependability, and authority that God's Word demands. We call this *verbal,* or *plenary inspiration,* which means that every word is inspired.

## What Is Inspiration?

In everyday language the term *inspiration* is used loosely. Poets and artists are said to be inspired as they write or paint. But their inspiration refers to a psychological state in which they feel more profoundly or see with greater clarity. Divine inspiration is much more than that.

The noted A. H. Strong defined inspiration as:

> A special divine influence on the minds of the writers of the Bible, in virtue of which their productions, apart from errors in transcription, and when rightly interpreted, together constitute an infallible rule of faith and practice.[1]

## The Breath of God

The word *inspired* comes from the Latin and means "in-breathed." Coming from two words, *in* and *spiro,* the word signifies "to blow and breathe in or into." God breathed into men that which men breathed out when He inspired them to write the Scriptures.

Let it be emphasized again. The Bible is not only

inspired, it is God-inspired; produced by the all-powerful breath of God. God inspired men (2 Samuel 23:2; 2 Peter 1:21) to give us an inspired Book (2 Timothy 3:16).

The personalities of the writers were not suppressed. As God breathed, there was active and conscious cooperation of the human and the divine. Every word was so controlled as to be inspired. The writer wasn't an instrument, but an agent. He wasn't a drugged or entranced medium, or a speaking robot. He was a joyful, conscious fellow worker with God. The vocabulary was that of the man. And thus we recognize the styles of Mark, Peter, James, and John.

Inspiration is that special act of the Holy Spirit by which He guided the writers so that their words conveyed the thoughts He wished to convey. The writers were so guided that their words related to the other inspired Books, and were free from errors of fact and doctrine and without omission.

While all of the faculties of thinking and uttering were so controlled as to be verbally infallible and inerrant, the Holy Spirit interpenetrated all of the human—the reasoning, the will, the emotions—so that the inspired utterance is guaranteed. The whole man was used—his style of utterance, his quality of mind, his emotional traits—God suiting the writer's abilities to His message.

## What Is Plenary Inspiration?

Plenary inspiration means that "all" was inspired. The word *plenary* comes from the Latin *plenus* meaning "full." All Scripture is inspired of God.

Jesus recognized the entire Old Testament when He spoke of the Law, the prophets, and the psalms (Luke 24:44). Paul called the Old Testament the

11

oracles of God (Romans 3:2). Peter ranked the words of Paul with Scripture (2 Peter 3:15, 16).

## What Is Verbal Inspiration?

Verbal means "word." Every word is inspired. The qualities of infallibility, inerrancy, and divine authority are attributes of the very words of the original manuscripts. At this point, we who believe in verbal inspiration are taunted by those who say our position is derogatory to God. We are told that verbal inspiration reduces the inspired person to a mechanical machine, much as a lifeless typewriter records the words touched off by the typist.

The writers were not robots. They were not passive; their faculties were active in recording God's message. The process was neither merely dictational nor mechanical. Someone said it well: "The gold was His; the mold was theirs." Involved was a mysterious interaction between the Spirit and the human authors.

Inspired Scripture—yet the heartthrobs of man. We find the cry of the human heart in need, repentance, prayer, praise, trust, and worship, as presented by the Holy Spirit. And we find ourselves lifted to God as we echo the feelings of the writers. This is supernatural and beyond description!

## How Did Inspiration Come?

The Holy Spirit revealed the hidden thoughts of God to men, then directed and controlled the writing of that revelation. We may not be able to theorize dogmatically on the methods employed by the Spirit, but the fact is plainly there for our acceptance.

Three methods seem to have been employed—superintendence, elevation, and suggestion.

1. *Superintendence* is divine guidance in the narration of facts and the facts to be narrated. This type of inspiration was in operation as the writers reported the things they had personally witnessed.

2. *Elevation* is that kind of inspiration that neither relates a narration of past events nor predicts future events. Examples are the sublime utterances in portions of the Book of Psalms, Job, and the Epistles.

3. *Suggestion.* One example will illustrate the many. How else could Matthew 9:21 quote the inner thoughts of the woman with the issue of blood? Sheer fancy, outright forgery, or divine inspiration? The infallible Scriptures can only be the latter.

## The Master's Voice

Have you noticed the old RCA label and emblem? There's a picture of a dog listening intently—head cocked, ears erect—to a record player. The slogan is "His Master's Voice." The Bible is "the Master's voice"; such is its function. It's not mechanically transcribed like a stereo record. Nevertheless, it's a record through which the Creator speaks to the creature. His words ring so distinctly that any person who will listen can hear the Master's voice.

Is it necessary to believe in verbal inspiration? The Church must have an objective standard to differentiate between true doctrine and false. True religion doesn't blunder, stumble, or falter on the guesses of men who evolve a man-made faith. If we are to know right from wrong, if we are to make heaven, we must have a clear word from God.

The doctrine of verbal inspiration brings us under the authority of our eternal God and His supernatural revelation. As a Bible-believing Christian, you have a foundation for your faith.

The statement, "Thus saith the Lord," or its equivalent, occurs over 2,500 times in the Old Testament alone. The Bible—every Book and every word—is the Word of God!

The Bible needs no one to defend it. But a rational statement of why we believe the Bible to be God's Word—His revelation to man, the one complete and infallible rule of faith and conduct—is important.

The Word of God is *authoritative.* It is the supreme authority in matters of faith and conduct (2 Timothy 3:16; 1 Thessalonians 2:13; 2 Peter 1:21).

The Bible is *infallible* (Psalm 119:140, 160). The Bible neither falsifies nor fails in its mission.

The Bible is *inerrant,* meaning it is free from error and is wholly true (Psalm 19:7-9; 119:89; Titus 1:2; 1 Peter 1:23, 25; John 10:35; Luke 16:17).

Dr. W. A. Criswell tells of a young fellow living in a large city with steep hills. He drove an old jalopy that needed a running start to make it up the hills. He had had this running start to make it up a particularly steep hill, but just as he came to the intersection at the bottom of the hill he discovered a car, followed by another, coming on the right. In seconds he made the decision. By letting the first one through and gunning his pile of junk he could get through ahead of the second. But what he didn't see was that the first was towing the second. They were tied together with a steel cable!

Dr. Criswell points out that the lad had learned this great theological lesson: it is very difficult to divide things that are bound together! Inspiration, infallibility, authority, and inerrancy are all bound together in God's written revelation, the Bible.

[1] Quoted by P. C. Nelson, "The Scripture Inspired," *Redemption Tidings*, April 26, 1963.

# 2

## One God . . . Three Persons

*Read:* Genesis 1:1; Deuteronomy 6:4; Matthew 28:19; John 1:1-18; Philippians 2:5-9; 1 John 3:23, 24; Revelation 5:1-7. *Key Verse:* "Hear, O Israel: The Lord our God is one Lord" (Deuteronomy 6:4). (See statements #2 and #3 on pp. 124, 125.)

Do you understand the doctrine of the Trinity? One fellow said: "I can't see how you can help but believe in the Trinity—you're a trinity yourself—body, soul, and spirit." Another illustrated the Trinity with the clover leaf which has three leaves within one.

Still another person remarked: "We're asked to believe that each of the three Persons of the Trinity is God, but then that the three are not three but one. How can you swallow that?"

Both the first man and the second were correct in their mathematics, but they were wrong in their doctrine. The third man was correct in his doctrine, but inaccurate in his math. How come? The first two made the mistake of failing to distinguish between things that are tripartite and God who is triune. The clover leaf has three petals but each petal is a third of the leaf, not the whole. The third fellow felt it was a needless and mystifying complication.

### One-third God?

When you pray, "Our Father . . . , you're not addressing one-third of God, but God himself.

15

In math the whole is equal to the sum of the parts. But with God, one part is equal to the whole. To not accept the doctrine of the Trinity is to lose sound theology; to try to comprehend the doctrine is to almost lose your wits. Little wonder the Psalmist declared: "Such knowledge is too wonderful for me; it is high, I cannot attain unto it" (Psalm 139:6), as he pondered God's omnipresence and omniscience.

## Bristling With Difficulties

No person can truly explain the Trinity. Down through the years scholars have propounded theories and presented assumptions to explore this mysterious Biblical doctrine. But despite their good efforts, the Trinity is still beyond human comprehension.

Bristling with difficulties, the doctrine of the Trinity makes up the keystone of the arch of evangelical faith. The Trinity defies logic and yet it's the hub of the wheel of Christian faith.

The doctrine of the Trinity, which we admit defies human reason, must be received as true on the authority of the Bible. It can't be made subject to logic. Man's corrupted reasoning is not the sole criterion for determining the truth of revelation. God's revelation can't be judged by man; nor can God's revelation be replaced by human reason.

The Trinity is revealed to us only in the Bible. God has chosen to reveal some things to us through nature and conscience. The Trinity, however, is not among them. This truth comes by supernatural revelation alone.

## How Can Three Be One?

We can only illustrate the Trinity by examples of

things that are tripartite, such as the trinity of body, soul, and spirit or the trinity of the body—head, trunk, and limbs. But there is a three-in-one pattern in the universe. Space, matter, and time are the basics of the universe. Each is a trinity.

*Space has three dimensions*—length, width, and height. Visualize a box 1 cubic foot in size. The dimensions are genuinely distinct. The length is not the width, and the width is not the height. But each of the three is essential to the other. Take any one away and you have a plane. Each of the dimensions is not a third of the cubic foot of space, but the whole. The three dimensions are a part one of the other. The space is 1 cubic foot, and this three-in-oneness is absolute. Each of the dimensions is the whole. Space couldn't exist in less than three dimensions.

*Time has three tenses*—past, present, and future. All of time has been future, all has been or will be present, all is or will be past. Each tense is distinct and yet is whole.

*Matter is composed of three things*—energy, motion, and phenomena—three modes of existence, distinct and yet one, and each is the whole.

A further example borrowed from an article by Gordon Harman will give additional clarity. In mathematics three ones do not necessarily make three: $1 \div 1 \div 1 = 1$ or $1 \times 1 \times 1 = 1$. But $1 + 1 + 1 = 3$. How do we know which math sign to use? The answer: when things indwell one another such as length, breadth, and height indwell space equally, you can only multiply them. The three Persons in the Godhead, though distinct, indwell one another reciprocally and we can only multiply them. The answer to the equation is one.

The basic teaching of the Scriptures, both Old and New Testaments, is the doctrine of the Trinity. You must take your stand on this doctrine if you are to view Scripture correctly. The doctrine of the Trinity is the doctrine of God that is characteristic of Christianity. Many religions profess a belief in God and even agree that He is the Creator. But when we assert our faith in Jesus Christ they part company with us. To deny the deity of Christ or the deity of the Holy Spirit is to leave you with theism that will never satisfy the mind or heart.

Although the word *trinity* is not in the Bible, it expresses a scriptural truth. The word is of Latin origin and means "three-in-one." Webster defines it as follows: "The union of three persons or hypostases (the Father, the Son, and the Holy Ghost) in one Godhead, so that all the three are one God as to substance, but three persons or hypostases as to individuality." This definition is correct, giving the exact teaching of both the Old and New Testaments.

## Three, Yet One

In his speech on Mars Hill, Paul made reference to the Godhead (Acts 17:29). The word translated *Godhead* may also be translated "that which is divine." In his letter to the Colossians the apostle declares that in Christ "dwelleth all the fullness of the Godhead bodily" (2:9). These two passages make it clear that Paul comprehended the Godhead to be all that is divine.

The word appearing in the Hebrew text of the Old Testament, which is usually translated *God* when applied to the true God, is plural. When this same word refers to idols or heathen gods, the English translation renders it *gods*. When the word refers to the true God, the translators always spell it *God*, as if it were a singular noun.

18

The Old Testament gives emphasis to the unity of God. Again and again there is the declaration that there is but one God. These assertions are made in contrast to the many false gods of the heathen. In an embryonic way the plurality of God is taught. The very frequent name for God as a Being of great power, *Elohim,* is plural. Pronouns for God as "us" (Genesis 1:26; 11:7; Isaiah 6:8) indicates plurality.

In the New Testament the doctrine is taught with utmost clarity. In fact, the doctrine is presupposed even more than it is expressly taught. The New Testament is founded on the doctrine of the Trinity. The incarnation of the Second Person of the Godhead and the work of the Third Person gave substance to the doctrine even before it was enunciated in words.

### First Announced

The Trinity was first announced when the birth of Jesus was announced. Every Hebrew knew that God is One. The fact that God is also three Persons was first fully revealed when the virgin Mary was told in the annunciation that she was to be the mother of the Son of God. The angel Gabriel came to Mary's simple home in Nazareth to declare: "The Holy Ghost shall come upon thee, and the power of the Highest shall overshadow thee: therefore also that holy thing which shall be born of thee shall be called the Son of God" (Luke 1:35).

### First Manifested

The Trinity was first manifested publicly at Jesus' baptism. The Son was "baptized, and praying"; the Holy Ghost "descended in a bodily shape"; and the Father spoke from the heavens: "Thou art my beloved Son; in thee I am well pleased" (3:21, 22).

Here the Trinity appeared, revealed both to the senses and the soul—the Father audibly, the Spirit visibly, and the Son visibly and audibly.

## First Explained

The Trinity was first explained by Jesus. In His conversations with His disciples in the Upper Room and en route to Gethsemane, the rich truth of the Trinity comes through simply and yet profoundly. The Son would pray the Father to give them the Spirit (John 14:16). All are eternal. All are God. All are Persons. All are One.

## First Formally Announced

The Trinity was first formally announced by Jesus. Perhaps the most famous passage of all is found in the Great Commission given by the risen Lord to His disciples: "Go ye therefore, and teach all nations, baptizing them in the name of the Father, and of the Son, and of the Holy Ghost" (Matthew 28:19). All three Persons of the Trinity are mentioned in the most complete equality and coordination. All three Persons, yet One. This passage establishes the creedal standard and confession of all Christian converts.

To believe in Jesus is to believe in the Trinity. To believe in God is to be a theist. To believe in Jesus as the only begotten Son of God and as your Saviour and Lord makes you a Christian. The deity of the Lord Jesus Christ hinges on the doctrine of the Trinity. He is the supreme evidence of the Trinity.

Many other New Testament passages clearly enunciate the Trinity. Foremost is the apostolic benediction of 2 Corinthians 13:14: "The grace of the Lord Jesus Christ, and the love of God, and the

communion of the Holy Ghost, be with you all."
Significantly, the word *Lord* in the Pauline epistles
is the Greek word used to translate the holy name of
God, "Jehovah," a clear designation of deity.

The Trinity was active in redemption (1 Peter 1:2;
Hebrews 10:7, 10, 15). The Trinity is active in the
giving of the Spirit (John 14:16; Acts 2:33; 1 Corinthians 12:4-6). The Trinity is active in our prayer life
(Ephesians 2:18; 1 John 2:1; John 14:16, 17; Romans
8:26). The Trinity is our example (John 17:21).

### Three Persons

The Statement of Fundamental Truths says:

> There is *that* in the Son which constitutes Him *the
> Son* and not the Father; and there is *that* in the Holy
> Ghost which constitutes Him *the Holy Ghost* and not
> either the Father or the Son. Wherefore the Father is
> the Begetter, the Son is the Begotten; and the Holy
> Ghost is the one proceeding from the Father and the
> Son. Therefore, because these three persons in the
> Godhead are in a state of unity, there is but one Lord
> God Almighty and His name one. John 1:18; 15:26;
> 17:11, 21; Zechariah 14:9.

Quoting further from the Statement of Fundamental Truths, we have this on the identity and cooperation in the Godhead:

> The Father, the Son, and the Holy Ghost are never
> *identical* as to *Person;* nor *confused* as to relation; nor
> *divided* in respect to the Godhead; nor *opposed* as to
> *cooperation.* The Son is *in* the Father and the Father is
> *in* the Son, as to relationship. The Son is *with* the Father
> and the Father is *with* the Son, as to fellowship. The
> Father is not *from* the Son, but the Son is *from* the
> Father, as to authority. The Holy Ghost is *from* the
> Father and the Son proceeding, as to nature, relation-
> ship, cooperation, and authority. Hence, neither Person

21

in the Godhead either exists or works separately or independently of the others. John 5:17-30, 32, 37; John 8:17, 18.

The Father is the Source of all—the absolute. He is unknown unless revealed by the Son (Matthew 11:27; John 1:18; 14:9). He is unapproachable except through the reconciliation of the Son (14:6).

The Second Person of the Trinity is the Son. The Son is the eternal Word, the Logos of God, who was God and was with God from eternity (John 1:2; Proverbs 8:22; Philippians 2:6; Colossians 1:18-21). Of like nature and possessing similar attributes, He is subordinate to the Father only in position. As the Executor of the Trinity in redemption, the Son fulfilled the redemptive plan of the Father.

The Holy Spirit is the present Agent of the Trinity in the world. He is a Person, and personality and powers are attributed to Him. He speaks. He wills. He is grieved. He does God's work in the world.

## Deviations From Trinitarian Doctrine

Through the centuries the doctrine of the Trinity has been assailed by various church leaders. There are five well-known groups today that as a part of their belief deny the Trinity. They are spiritism, Christian Science, Unitarianism, Jehovah's Witnesses, and Christadelphians.

Following the apostolic days there were those who espoused *tritheism*. They believed in three separate individual gods.

The third century saw two main camps of deviation. *Arianism*, named after Arius, a church leader of the day, propounded the doctrine that Christ, though preexistent before His incarnation was a created being and therefore not eternal and divine. This is the teaching of Jehovah's Witnesses in our day.

*Sabellianism* takes its name from Bishop Sabellius who argued that Father, Son, and Holy Spirit are not three eternally existent Persons, but simply three aspects or manifestations of God. The modern "Jesus Only" teaching is a form of this error.

*Unitarianism* holds to the Oneness of God, but reduces Christ to an ethical teaching. The modern liberal and the existentialist are in this category. All, in essence, deny the personality of God.

### Let's Summarize

Let's summarize the doctrine of the Trinity:

1. There is only one God (Deuteronomy 6:4; 1 Timothy 2:5; James 2:19).
2. He is in three Persons—Father, Son, and Holy Spirit (Luke 1:35; 3:21, 22; John 14:16; Matthew 28:19; 2 Corinthians 13:14).
3. The Father is God (1 Peter 1:2; John 6:27).
4. The Son is God (Hebrews 1:8; John 1:1; 20:28).
5. The Holy Spirit is God (Acts 5:3, 4; 1 Corinthians 3:16).
6. Each of the Three is essential to the others.
7. Each of the Three is the whole.
8. The three Persons indwell one another.
9. All Three are equal, almighty, and eternal.

With respect to our redemption, the Father thought it, the Son bought it, and the Spirit wrought it. The Father adopts us, provides for our needs, and disciplines us. The Son succors us in our weaknesses, trials, and temptations. The Spirit indwells, teaches, guides, and strengthens us.

# 3
## Man—His Fall and Salvation

*Read:* Genesis 1:26, 27; 3:4-6; Psalm 8:4-8; Romans 3:21-25; 5:11-19; 1 Peter 1:18, 19. *Key Verse:* "The Spirit itself beareth witness with our spirit, that we are the children of God" (Romans 8:16). (See statements #4 and #5 on p. 126.)

The setting is a lumber mill in timber country. The foreman orders a crooked, gnarled log to be run through the giant saw. The log comes out in straight dimensions, but the grain in every board is crooked and each board is weakened with an excessive number of knots.

How like fallen man. He may say, "I'm going to cut out lying. I'll saw off cheating. I'll rip off swearing. I'll straighten out on my carousing." Cut out these habits and he'll still be just as crooked in his heart.

All men are sinners. There are no exceptions. Born in the evil corruption and guilt of original sin—the source of all personal acts of sin—every individual stands in need of salvation from sin. There are many who would deny the reality of sin. But the evidence is so overwhelming that denial is absurd to any thinking person.

### Daily Reminders

Every hospital, funeral home, and cemetery is a testimony to the Fall. Pain, disease, and death are results of the Fall.

Every locked door, bank vault, and burglar alarm

24

is evidence of the Fall. Every policeman, court trial, and prison indicates the fall of man. Sin has blighted, twisted, wrecked, and destroyed until no one can deny its existence.

The Statement of Fundamental Truths says:

> Man was created good and upright . . . in [God's] image. . . . However, man by voluntary transgression fell and thereby incurred not only physical death but also spiritual death, which is separation from God.

## God Said, "Very Good"

The Bible introduces the first man and the woman God provided to be his helpmate, in the simplest and most intelligent words possible (Genesis 1:26, 27; 2:7, 18-25). After God created the other parts of His universe He pronounced His work "good." But after He had formed man, God declared His work "very good."

Man was created in the image of God. This image or likeness was not a physical resemblance since God is Spirit and does not have a physical body. The likeness was moral. Adam had spiritual faculties. He was created good and upright, with a conscience and a will. Man was also endowed with intelligence and reason. Created a "little lower than the angels" (Psalm 8:4-8), man was lifted far above any other creature.

God placed man in a paradise of harmony, peace, and happiness. Adam and Eve enjoyed face-to-face communion with God. All was ideal.

However, as part of being made in the image of God, man was also given the power to choose. He could choose between good and evil, between obedience and disobedience. God wanted beings who would in love and freedom choose to worship and serve Him.

Man was put on probation after Creation, but he is not on probation now. Created with tendencies toward God, man was also susceptible to temptation. There was no need for disobedience in Eden. Adam and Eve had plenty, and when they did eat, it was not a matter of necessity.

Many today blame God for sending people to hell, but God never sends anyone to hell. People go there of their own free choice.

The reason God put the temptation in the Garden was to test the virtues of our first parents. God had the right to command; Adam and Eve had the responsibility to obey. Temptation didn't necessitate a fall. The ability not to sin would have become the inability to sin. God's "thou shalt not" recognized the possibility that Adam and Eve could disobey.

## The Tragic Choice

Disobey they did. Eve first, and then Adam, sinned by partaking of the forbidden fruit. Immediately their fellowship with God was broken. Shame and fear came on them. Before they had had a holy fear of God in the sense of reverential awe. Now there was fear of judgment. Spiritual death resulted and the sentence of physical death came too. The curse of degradation was also part of God's judgment (Genesis 3:14-19).

The consequences of the Fall were far-reaching. All creation came under God's curse. Since all descendants of Adam share his guilt (Romans 5:12), all his posterity without exception are under the penalty and condemnation of death (3:23). Man's nature—morally, mentally, and spiritually—was perverted. Sinful man loves what God hates and hates what God loves. He has a sinful nature.

If the source of a city's water supply has in some manner become contaminated, every outlet in the system is endangered until the poison has been removed. Through the pollution of Adam, the head of the race, the entire human race has become contaminated with the poison of sin.

Sin is *rebellion* against the government of God. Sin is *refusal* to submit to the will of God. Sin is *defiance* of God. Sin is an *attitude* toward the government of heaven. Sin, and only sin, *separates* men from God. God can't look on sin. And the sinner is unable to get back to God by any effort of his own (Titus 3:5).

Sin brings a deep and terrible sense of guilt and condemnation to our innermost being. How can you rid yourself of this horrible load? One of the most frequent suggestions is to deny that there is such a thing as sin and guilt. But it just doesn't work!

## On Legs and Tails

Once Abraham Lincoln was asked, "How many legs would a sheep have if you counted his tail as a leg?" Lincoln's simple but brilliant answer was, "Four. Counting a tail as a leg doesn't make it one!" Sin is sin regardless of what you call it or how much you deny it.

The divine indictment stands—"All have sinned." We are sinners by nature and by deliberate choice. We are sinners in God's sight (Romans 3:9-20).

What shall we do? There is no hope for us outside of divine grace. We're like Lady Macbeth in Shakespeare's famous sleep-walking scene. She tries to wash imaginary drops of blood from her hands as she cries out, "All the perfumes of Arabia will not sweeten this little hand."

27

There's hope—hope through God. He is "not willing that any should perish, but that all should come to repentance" (2 Peter 3:9).

## Lost . . . Regained

We lost it all in the first Adam; but, thank God, He sent the Last Adam, the Lord Jesus Christ. Through Him we can regain it all. For "where sin abounded, grace did much more abound" (Romans 5:20).

The holiness of God excuses no sin, but the love of God forgives all sin through the Lord Jesus Christ. While pronouncing judgment on sin in Eden, God announced the way of forgiving and restoring lost man—a blood way, prefigured by the slain animal (Genesis 3:15, 21).

"Man's only hope of redemption is through the shed blood of Jesus Christ the Son of God"—so reads the Statement of Fundamental Truths. The Bible states that we are redeemed with "the precious blood of Christ" (1 Peter 1:19) and the "blood of Jesus Christ his Son cleanseth us from all sin" (1 John 1:7).

In 1927 a West African national named Asibi was sick with yellow fever. A blood specimen was taken from him. Since that year all the vaccine manufactured by the government, the Rockefeller Foundation, and other agencies has come from the original strain of virus taken from Asibi's veins. Millions the world over have been immunized through the repeated cultures in the laboratories of country after country. In a real sense, the blood of one man has served the human race. But how much more has been the value of the blood of Christ. Christ's precious blood can accomplish the miracle of cleansing us from sin.

A Philippian jailor centuries ago cried out, "What must I do to be saved?" (Acts 16:30). The answer then was: "Believe on the Lord Jesus Christ, and thou shalt be saved." The solution still holds good today. But you must be willing, for God forces none against his will.

## Conditions to Salvation

Salvation is the theme of the entire Bible. It's at the heart of every gospel sermon and every hymn.

In his book *Bible Doctrines,* P. C. Nelson presents the conditions of salvation as follows:[1]

1. Salvation is from God, not man (Luke 3:6).

2. Salvation is through Christ alone (Acts 4:12).

3. Salvation is obtained by grace and not by works (Ephesians 2:8-10).

4. Salvation is for the whole man (Isaiah 53:1-10; Romans 8:19-23).

5. Salvation is for time and eternity (Ephesians 2:8; Hebrews 5:9). Salvation is in three tenses—past, present, and future. We have been saved from the penalty of sin (2 Corinthians 2:15; Ephesians 1:7; 2:5, 8; 2 Timothy 1:9). We are being saved from the power of sin (Romans 6:14; 2 Corinthians 8:18; Philippians 2:12, 13). We will be saved from the presence of sin (Romans 13:11; Philippians 3:20, 21; 1 Peter 1:5).

6. Salvation is neglected at fearful cost (Hebrews 2:1-4; 10:28, 29).

7. Faith in Christ as our crucified and risen Saviour and Lord is the procuring cause of salvation (John 3:14-36; 5:24).

8. The Father, Son, and Holy Spirit cooperate with the sinner in his salvation.

## Two Sides to Salvation

There are two sides to salvation—*God's part* and *our part*. God's work finds expression in five words: atonement, propitiation, substitution, redemption, and reconciliation.

## Christ Atoned for Our Sins

The English word *atonement* occurs 76 times in the Old Testament and once in the New (Romans 5:11). Invariably, the word means covering. The sacrificial death of Jesus Christ makes forgiveness available to you and me. His shed blood is the vital atoning principle. "Without shedding of blood is no remission" of sin (Hebrews 9:22).

A Christian lady lay dying. A minister called on her, announcing that he had come to grant her absolution. "Absolution," she repeated, "what is that?" "Forgiveness of sins," he replied. "Oh, how wonderful," she said. "Please let me see your hand."

The minister gave her his hand. She took it and looked for some time at the palm. Then she cried out, "Imposter! The One who has forgiven my sins has the print of the nail in his hand."

## Christ Is Our Propitiation

The word *propitiation* (Romans 3:25) means to bring together, to make favorable. God the Father accepted the propitiatory gift of His Son and thus makes provision to restore us to His love.

## Christ Became Our Substitute

Christ did for us on the cross what we couldn't do for ourselves (Isaiah 53). We are accepted in Him (Ephesians 1:6).

## Christ Redeemed Us

The word *redeemed* means to buy back by paying a price. The Bible declares that we were redeemed with the precious blood of Christ (1 Peter 1:18, 19). His blood is the red coin by which our salvation was purchased.

Never minimize the word *blood,* any more than you would minimize its value in the realm of modern medicine. People talk about "blood money" and "blood feuds." Churchill made famous the words "blood, sweat, toil, and tears." The medical world speaks of blood pressure, blood transfusions, and blood classifications. Doctors take blood tests, and police officers investigate blood stains.

How unreasonable to stress the value of human blood and despise the blood of Christ shed on Calvary to bring life to lost sinners. A dying person doesn't receive life by looking at the fittest man in the community; his life is saved by accepting blood plasma. We're not redeemed by the beautiful example of Jesus' life, but by His shed blood.

## Christ Reconciled Us

Through Christ we have been *reconciled.* Sin had separated us from God, but "we were reconciled to God by the death of his Son" (Romans 5:10).

## Man's Part

We can't save ourselves (Ephesians 2:8, 9). But there is something for us to do.

1. *We need to repent.* Repentance is the translation of two New Testament Greek words. One expresses the emotional element and means regret. The other means a change of mind, carrying with it

the idea of will. Repentance is godly sorrow for sin with sincere effort to forsake it. Repentance concerns the intellect (Matthew 21:28-30), the emotions (2 Corinthians 7:9, 10), and the will (Luke 15:18-20).

2. *We need to exercise faith.* Faith means belief and trust, the assent of the mind and the consent of the will (Romans 10:9, 10). Faith is based on knowledge, dependable evidence. Saving faith is the acceptance by the intellect, the emotions, and the will, of God's salvation extended to us through Christ.

## Three Aspects of Salvation

There are three aspects of salvation, each referring to a different act on the part of God. They are *regeneration, justification,* and *sanctification.*

*Regeneration* is that change wrought by the Spirit of God by which you become a new creature in Christ (John 3:1-13). Another expression is *conversion,* which is the turning of the sinner from his sins unto God for salvation. It is not accomplished by reformation, resolutions, church membership, or turning over a new leaf. Regeneration comes by the *new birth.* It's not the altering, reforming, or reinvigorating of the old nature (2 Corinthians 5:17).

*Justification* is the judicial act of God by which He pronounces the believing sinner righteous, freeing him from condemnation, and restoring him to divine favor (Romans 3:24).

D. L. Moody uniquely illustrated God's gift of righteousness by the penitent thief:

The thief on the cross had nails through both hands, so that he could not work, and a nail through each foot, so that he could not run errands for the Lord; he could not lift a hand or a foot toward his salvation; and yet Christ offered him the gift of God, and he took it. He threw him a passport and took him with Him into Paradise.

*Sanctification* is the process that separates a sinner from the secular and sinful and sets him apart for sacred purposes (Romans 6). The word is synonymous with holiness and consecration. Sanctification is in a sense instantaneous, for the moment we believe in Christ we are separated from sin and unto God. Sanctification is also progressive. Christ is our Sanctification, the Holy Spirit is the Sanctifier, and we are the sanctified.

## How Can I Know I Am Saved?

Evidences of salvation are both *inward* and *outward.* Inward evidences are: (1) the witness of the Holy Spirit (Romans 8:16); (2) the sense of a lifted load (Psalm 32:3-6); (3) the joy of salvation (51:12); (4) love for other Christians (1 John 3:14); and (5) the sense of the Holy Spirit's leadership (Romans 8:14).

Outward evidences are: (1) a changed life (2 Corinthians 5:17); (2) a desire to keep God's commandments (1 John 2:3); and (3) ability to overcome the world (5:4).

Two plus two equals four—that's mathematics—count and see. Hydrogen and oxygen in proper proportions make water—that's science—taste and see. "Believe on the Lord Jesus Christ and thou shalt be saved"—that's salvation—try it and see. In God's Word I read it. In the experience of my soul I know it.

---

[1] P. C. Nelson, *Bible Doctrines* (Springfield, MO: Gospel Publishing House, rev. ed., 1971), pp. 46-54.

# 4
## The Two Ordinances

*Read:* 1 Peter 3:18-21; 1 Corinthians 10:1, 2; 11:26-29; Colossians 2:11, 12; Matthew 28:19; Romans 6:1-11. *Key Verses:* "Go ye therefore, and teach all nations, baptizing them in the name of the Father, and of the Son, and of the Holy Ghost: teaching them to observe all things whatsoever I have commanded you" (Matthew 28:19, 20). (See statement #6 on p. 126.)

We believe that our Lord commanded the observance of two ordinances—water baptism and the Lord's Supper. Water baptism speaks of spiritual life begun and the observance of the Lord's Supper speaks of spiritual life continued. Both are acts of obedience that are important to maintaining fellowship with Christ.

### Water Baptism

A father and mother were about to be baptized in water. Their little son, unfamiliar with religious terminology, proudly announced, "Mom and Dad are going to be advertised tonight." The boy's word choice was wrong, but in a sense it wasn't all that bad. All believers who obey this command of Christ truly advertise their Christian faith.

Beliefs regarding the ordinances vary among church groups. Some practice several in addition to water baptism and the Lord's Supper.

The Roman Catholic church believes that baptism

and penance are essential to salvation. Another five sacraments are helpful, providing additional means for the grace of God to provide salvation.

Another segment of the church world, such as the Quakers and the Salvation Army, believes the inward reality of Christ precludes the need of visible signs. As a result, they observe neither the Lord's Supper nor water baptism.

A large section of the church world teaches that by baptism a person is brought into the benefits of the Christian covenant. Some of these believe that it only becomes fruitful when faith and obedience are exercised. Baptism, according to this general view, may precede faith.

Still another large segment believes that the ordinances are strictly for believers. Baptism is not for infants or for unbelievers.

Several questions are raised whenever water baptism is discussed: (1) What is the Biblical method of baptism? (2) What is the right formula for administering the ordinance? (3) What is the meaning or significance of the observance? (4) Who qualifies for baptism?

Baptism is a fundamental issue. To despise this scriptural rite is to despise the ordinance of God. That it is important is underscored by the fact that Christ himself was baptized in the Jordan, declaring: "Thus it becometh us to fulfill all righteousness" (Matthew 3:15).

## The Biblical Method

While baptism is generally practiced among all churches, there is a wide variety in mode and meaning. A controversy settles in at these two points.

The word *baptize* means literally "to dip" or "to

immerse." No stretch of the imagination can make baptism mean less. Significantly, there are eight words in the Greek New Testament used to describe the application of liquids. With this wide choice of words meaning "sprinkle," "pour," and "immerse," only the one meaning "immerse" is used for water baptism. The word *baptize* is found 74 times in the New Testament.

The Bible gives these significant statements regarding baptism:

1. Water is required. "And as they went on their way, they came unto a certain water: and the eunuch said, See, here is *water;* what doeth hinder me to be baptized?" (Acts 8:36).

2. Much water is needed. John baptized in "Aenon . . . because there was *much water* there" (John 3:23). Sprinkling wouldn't require much.

3. Both the candidate and the administrator went down into the water. "And they went *down both into the water*" (Acts 8:38).

4. In baptism we are buried. "We are *buried* with him by baptism into death" (Romans 6:4). (See also Colossians 2:12.) To bury anything means to cover it.

5. The candidate comes up out of the water. "And Jesus, when he was baptized, *went up straightway out of the water*" (Matthew 3:16). "And when they were *come up out of the water,* . . ." (Acts 8:39).

## Testimony of the Reformers

Martin Luther (on page 176 in his Large Catechism published in Norway) states:

> But the symbol or outward act is this, that we dip down into the water so that it goes over us, and then coming up out of it again. Here are two acts: to sink under the water and again to come up, which signifies

its symbol, which is nothing else than the death of old Adam, and the resurrection of the new man. . . .

John Calvin, in discussing the proper scriptural mode of baptizing, said: "The very word 'baptize,' however, signifies to immerse; and it is certain that immersion was the practice of the ancient church."

## The Biblical Formula

"Baptizing them in the name of the Father, and of the Son, and of the Holy Ghost" (Matthew 28:19). Does this contradict Peter's command in Acts 2:38? There we read: "Be baptized every one of you in the name of Jesus Christ."

The latter verse does not lay down a formula, but rather describes the reason and purpose of baptism, acknowledging Jesus to be Christ and Lord.

P. C. Nelson comments in *Bible Doctrines:*[1]

We are not left to speculate on the proper formula, *"into* the name of the Father, and of the Son, and of the Holy Spirit." The American Revised, as well as Worrell's translation, has *into*, instead of *in*, and this is the correct translation from the Greek. Into fellowship with the name of the Holy Trinity. And we do this in the name of (by the authority and command of) Jesus Christ.

## The Biblical Meaning

Baptism presents three important truths:

1. *The gospel is proclaimed.* First Corinthians 15:3, 4 defines the gospel: "How that Christ died for our sins according to the Scriptures; and that he was buried, and that he rose again the third day according to the Scriptures."

Baptism, like the Lord's Supper, shows the Lord's death. The work of Christ on Calvary and the Resurrection are recited. The cleansing from sin is symbolized. The public sees what you believe.

2. *Our experience is pictured.* Baptism portrays conversion. "Old things are passed away; . . . all things are become new" (2 Corinthians 5:17). We portray our identification with Christ in a spiritual death, burial, and resurrection (Romans 6:4, 5; Colossians 2:12).

3. *Our hope is declared.* We state our belief in the resurrection from the dead. Jesus said: "Because I live, ye shall live also" (John 14:19).

## Who Can Be Baptized?

The Bible's answer is very simple. The sinner must first repent and believe (Mark 1:15; Acts 2:38). The New Testament teaches that only *believers* should be baptized. In every instance the test is individual faith. For example, Philip told the eunuch: "You can . . . if you believe with all your heart" (Acts 8:37, *Living Bible*).

What about infant baptism? There must be a personal sense of need, of guilt, before there can be an act of saving faith. Children, until they come to the age of accountability, are not expected to exercise saving faith. An infant can't repent, can't be converted, and can't believe in Jesus. Scripturally, they are excluded from baptism as are unbelievers. There is no command in the Bible for baptizing infants; neither is there an example.

## When Should Baptism Occur?

Christians have no choice but to obey the command of Christ. Satan tries to make us disobey. Prompt obedience will strengthen your Christian conscience.

F. F. Bruce, one of the finest New Testament scholars of our time, states that "the idea of an unbaptized Christian is simply not entertained in the New Testament." Baptism ought to be the "first of all outwardly duties" of the new Christian.

The Ethiopian official was baptized immediately (Acts 8:36-38). Paul was baptized by Ananias within hours after conversion. Cornelius and his houseful of friends obeyed the Lord in baptism the very day that saving faith came (10:47, 48). Lydia and her household were baptized shortly after conversion (16:14, 15). The Philippian jailor and his household were baptized that same hour (v. 33).

In the face of such overwhelming evidence, how can we postpone baptism after conversion? Peter preached, "Repent and be baptized."

## The Lord's Supper

Frequently a young man stands before the church altar and gives a ring to a young woman, saying words that mean, "This is for you." The ring may be a very ordinary gold band. There may be thousands like it the nation over. But for the girl who receives it, there is no other like it anywhere. It's for her. And to her it's not just a piece of jewelry to adorn her finger. That ring is the symbol of the greatest earthly gift she has ever received—the gift of a young man and his love " 'til death do us part." The gift of the ring says, "This is for you with all my love—my whole self with all that I have."

What a difference between looking at a row of rings in a jewelry store window and receiving this special ring with the words, "This is for you." There's a difference between knowing that love and commitment exist, and experiencing it personally.

The *New English Bible* translates 1 Corinthians 11:24 thus: "[Jesus] after giving thanks to God, broke it and said, 'This is my body, which is for you; do this as a memorial of me.'"

The Lord's Supper must not be abstract and general. Our Christian experience must move our hearts and vitally affect our daily behavior. Let us hear the Lord say, "This is for you."

We can be caught up with a maze of activities in our church life—activities that are necessary and proper. But just as we need the spiritual strength received through prayer and Bible reading, we need to rightly understand and receive spiritual strength in the Communion service. By faith we can appropriate Christ's work at Calvary for ourselves.

We share with Christ in the shedding of His blood and the breaking of His body at the Lord's Table (1 Corinthians 10:16). The word *communion* means "the act of sharing, or holding in common, participation."

### An Empty Cup

Too often we miss the rich reward to be found in a spiritual experience because we fail to understand the reality of spiritual truth. We're like the lady who attended a Communion service for the first time. When the tray passed her, she reached out and took an empty cup. Not only did she fail to get anything out of the cup, she also failed to get anything out of the service, for it was meaningless to her.

Yes, it's possible to get "an empty cup" when you partake at the Lord's Table, if you don't realize what it really means. True Christian faith does not thrive on ignorance.

# What Means the Supper?

The answer will both epitomize and express one's whole spiritual outlook. To the Roman Catholic it means to literally eat the Lord's body. This is called transubstantiation.

When the priest consecrates the bread and wine, they are believed to be changed into "the body and blood together with the soul and divinity" of Christ. Christ is sacrificed "for the living and the dead" every time the mass is celebrated. The consecrated bread and wine are worshiped and adored as Christ himself, and sacramental grace is believed to be conveyed. The bread is given to the laity, while the priests partake of both bread and wine.

The Lutheran view rejects transubstantiation but accepts consubstantiation. This means that the glorified body of Christ is not only in heaven, but everywhere, and especially, "under, in, and with" the bread and wine at the Lord's Table.

# What Do We Believe?

The Statement of Fundamental Truths of the Assemblies of God affirms:

> The Lord's Supper, consisting of the elements—bread and the fruit of the vine—is the symbol expressing our sharing the divine nature of our Lord Jesus Christ (2 Peter 1:4); a memorial of His suffering and death (1 Corinthians 11:26); and a prophecy of His second coming (1 Corinthians 11:26); and is enjoined on all believers "till He come!"

The language of the Statement is simple—a symbol, a memorial, a prophecy, and an enjoinder—the meaning is significantly rich.

41

# Baptism—Primary; Communion—Perpetual

Whereas water baptism is to be observed once by all believers, Communion is to be observed perpetually. Observe four descriptive words (1 Corinthians 11:23-29):

1. *Remembering.* "In remembrance of me." Two things are to be remembered. First, an event—the historical fact of the death of Christ. His blood was shed. Separate your blood from your body and you die. Christ died. His shed blood—and His alone—atoned for your sins and mine.

Second, we remember an experience—that Christ's death became actual and meaningful to the participant. This is the meaning of "eat" and "drink." The event must become an experience. The remembrance of the event without an experience is meaningless ceremony.

2. *Sustaining.* "Eat . . . drink." Eating and drinking are the most significant physical acts of life. What we eat and drink becomes part of ourselves. The language is charming in its simplicity—food and drink, the oldest language in the world. And it employs the three senses: sight, taste, and touch.

We are sustained as we feed on Christ. His teachings feed the intellect; His love feeds the emotions; His designs feed the will. Spiritual nourishment, fellowship, and healing are to be found at the Lord's Table.

3. *Examining.* "Let a man examine himself." Not his belief or his faith, but himself. The fellow who couldn't remember the sermon was asked, "What good did it do you?" "Well," he replied, "I went home and took the false bottom out of my bushel basket." That's it—not how much we remember, but how much we practice.

4. *Expecting.* "Till he come." The feast is limited in duration and purpose. We now walk by faith in an invisible, ascended Lord. But memory at the Lord's Table not only recalls the past, it enlarges expectation. The Lord's Supper is a reminder of the Lord's return. Faith will then give place to sight; hope to realization; promise to fulfillment. Bread and the fruit of the vine are the symbols now. But they will vanish away when the Lord himself is in our midst.

All too often we preach and pray about Christ in past tense. We even pitch songs in a minor key, as though He lived and died far away and long ago. We need to look on the Christ of the cross in the light that streams from His resurrection glory. And we look for Him to come again with joyous anticipation!

---

[1] Nelson, *op. cit.,* pp. 61, 62.

# 5
## *Power From on High*

*Read:* Luke 24:49; Acts 1:1-11; 2:1-39. *Key Verse:*
"But ye shall receive power, after that the Holy
Ghost is come upon you: and ye shall be witnesses
unto me both in Jerusalem, and in all Judea, and in
Samaria, and unto the uttermost part of the earth"
(Acts 1:8). (See statement #7 on pp. 126, 127.)

At the beginning of His earthly ministry Christ
gave constant emphasis to the Cross. As He drew
near to the end of His earthly ministry He emphasized the coming of the Holy Spirit. In private
conversation with His disciples just before going to
Calvary, Jesus spoke much of the promised Comforter (John 14; 16). Just before His ascension, He said:
"And, behold, I send the promise of my Father upon
you: but tarry ye in the city of Jerusalem, until ye be
endued with power from on high" (Luke 24:49); and,
"Ye shall receive power, after that the Holy Ghost is
come upon you" (Acts 1:8).

### Who Is He?

Who is the promised Holy Spirit? None other than
the Third Person of the Trinity. The full manifestation of His personality and deity, the meaning of
His equal position in the Godhead, and the scope
of His work, are declared in the New Testament.

### It Does Make a Difference

Whether the Holy Spirit is a Person and God of

very God, or a power that God the Father exerts in our lives makes all the difference in the world.

If you think of the Spirit as an influence or power, you'll think of Him as a force that you can capture and manipulate. If you think of the Spirit as the Scriptures present Him, you'll think of Him as a Person who is to get hold of you and use you. It's not for you to get the Holy Spirit to use Him, but for Him to get you and use you.

## His Name

In the Old Testament the Holy Spirit is spoken of as the Lord God (Isaiah 61:1). In the New Testament Peter accuses Ananias of lying to the Spirit, which he declares is a lie to God (Acts 5:3, 4). The deity of the Spirit is clearly stated by Paul (2 Corinthians 3:17).

## His Attributes

The attributes of deity—omnipotence, omniscience, omnipresence—are ascribed to the Spirit (Hebrews 9:14; 1 Corinthians 2:10, 11; Luke 1:35; Psalm 139:7-10). The Spirit is linked with the Father and the Son in the baptismal formula (Matthew 28:19) and the apostolic benediction (2 Corinthians 13:14). In the latter, the Spirit is placed equally with the Father and the Son in the singular name of God.

## His Works

The works of the Spirit declare His deity—in *creation* (Genesis 1:2; Psalm 104:30); *inspiration* (2 Peter 1:20, 21; 2 Timothy 3:16); *regeneration* (John 3:5, 6; Titus 3:5); *conviction* (John 16:8-11; Genesis 6:3); *baptism* (1 Corinthians 12:13); *sealing* (Ephesians 1:13; 4:30); and *sanctification* (2 Thessalonians 2:13; Galatians 5:22, 23).

## Is the Holy Spirit a Person?

To be a person one must have intellect, which is the ability to know; emotion, which is the ability to feel; and will, which is the ability to direct. Only persons think, speak, and will. These are the marks of God the Father and God the Son, and they are the marks of God the Spirit.

The Spirit's intellect is seen in 1 Corinthians 2:10, 11; His emotion is manifested in Ephesians 4:30; and His will is demonstrated in 1 Corinthians 12:11.

The Spirit has all the attributes and powers of the divine personality. He *speaks* (2 Samuel 23:1, 2; Acts 1:16; 28:25); *works wonders* (2:4; 8:39); *commands* and *forbids* (8:29; 10:19, 20; 13:2; 16:6, 7); *appoints* (20:28); *wills* (1 Corinthians 12:11); *foretells* (Acts 20:22, 23); *witnesses* (Romans 8:16); *aids* (v. 26); and *reveals* (1 Corinthians 2:9-12).

Possessing sensibilities as a Person, the Spirit can be *grieved* (Ephesians 4:30); *resisted* (Acts 7:51); *blasphemed* (Mark 3:29); and *lied to* (Acts 5:3). These are human responses to a Person, not a mere force.

## The Divine Executive

The Spirit is the Executive of the Godhead. He executes the designs of the Father and the purposes of the Son. He never speaks of himself, but declares what is said to Him by the Son (John 16:13, 14).

Throughout Scripture the Spirit is associated with the Father and Son with an equality of being, position, and responsibility (Matthew 28:19; 1 Corin-

thians 12:4-6; 2 Corinthians 13:14; Revelation 1:4).
For reasons unrelated to position or ability, the Son
is given second place and the Spirit the third in the
order in which the title of God is stated in the Bible.

Because the Holy Spirit is God, we ought always to
revere and obey Him. Because He indwells us, we
ought to cherish and honor Him. As our Teacher, we
may depend on Him for all spiritual knowledge. We
can rely on Him to supply our needs and depend on
Him for every spiritual good.

### When Do You Have the Holy Spirit?

The moment you accept Christ as your personal
Saviour the Holy Spirit takes up His residence in
your heart (Romans 8:9; 1 Corinthians 6:19).

To have the Spirit dwelling within, is to have One
who knows everything about you—your sins, fears,
tensions, inhibitions, struggles, hopes, and yearn-
ings. He is able to deal adequately with sin and
master it from inside. This is His work of sanctifying
you (Romans 6; 8). From the Spirit will come the
strength to live a Christlike life (Ephesians
3:16, 17, 20; Philippians 2:13; Galatians 4:6).

### Are All Spirit-filled?

We are born of the Spirit, transformed by the
Spirit, led by the Spirit, strengthened by the Spirit,
and we can be filled with the Spirit.

While the Holy Spirit indwells all true believers
(Romans 8:9), it does not follow that all believers are
Spirit-filled. Believers are baptized into the body of
Christ by the Holy Spirit; the Holy Spirit is the
agent. On the other hand, Christ is the agent who
baptizes us with the Holy Spirit (Matthew 3:11; John

47

1:33; Acts 2:33; Luke 24:49). This experience is called the "promise of [the] Father."

## Two Events

Peter's sermon at Pentecost evidences a concept of two separate events: (1) "Repent and be baptized...," and, (2) "ye shall receive the gift of the Holy Ghost" (Acts 2:38). The converts at Samaria believed and were baptized but received the baptism in the Holy Spirit later (8:12, 17). The same was true of the converts at Ephesus (Acts 19).

Three simple statements bring the matter of the Holy Spirit and the believer into focus.

*First,* the Holy Spirit indwells every believer. Through the initial operation of the Spirit the mysterious change, the new birth, takes place.

*Second,* the fullness of the Spirit has not been experienced by every believer.

*Third,* the fullness of the Spirit may be experienced by every believer. This is the baptism in the Holy Spirit.

## It's an Experience!

To be filled with the Spirit is to experience that which 120 obedient followers of the Lord Jesus Christ experienced when "they were all filled with the Holy Ghost, and began to speak with other tongues, as the Spirit gave them utterance" (Acts 2:4).

That experience on the Day of Pentecost was a great day in the annals of the Church. That which had been prophesied by Joel about 800 years before was fulfilled. The words of John the Baptist of 3 years earlier were now reality. The promise of Jesus to send the Comforter was no longer a future event.

The 120 had obeyed the Lord's command. Now His promise was fulfilled. What a life-changing experience!

## Who May Receive This Baptism?

"For the promise is unto you, and to your children, and to all that are afar off, even as many as the Lord our God shall call" (Acts 2:39). That was Peter's declaration at Pentecost. And, thank God, the promise has never been revoked.

I have seen people of every race baptized in the Holy Spirit. I have seen many young boys and girls gloriously filled. At other times the recipients were well beyond 70 years of age.

The Scriptures teach that the Baptism is for all believers (John 7:37-39). Jesus said, "If any man. . . ." Obviously He meant all when He stated, "He that believeth on me. . . ." All are included; none is excluded.

## Is It for You?

The promise is very personal; it is *to you*. The personal pronoun appears again and again. "*He* that believeth . . . out of *his* belly shall flow rivers of living water" (John 7:38). "The Father . . . shall give *you* another Comforter" (14:16). "He dwelleth with *you*, and shall be in *you*" (v. 17). "It is expedient for *you* . . . I will send him [the Comforter] unto *you*" (16:7). "He will guide *you* . . . and show *you*" (v. 13). "I send the promise of my Father upon *you*: but tarry *ye* . . . until *ye* be endued with power from on high" (Luke 24:29). "For the promise is unto *you*, and *your* children" (Acts 2:39).

## Is the Baptism a Luxury?

The Baptism is thought by some people to be a luxury rather than a necessity. They consider the experience to be desirable but optional.

The Scriptures indicate beyond all doubt that all believers are to receive. The 120 in the Upper Room seized upon the great words of Joel's prophecy, "upon all flesh." Joel included men and women, young and old alike. The promise went beyond the apostles; 108 additional persons received on the Day of Pentecost. Gentiles were included, much to the amazement of Peter and his party (Acts 10:45, 46).

Note again these Biblical expressions: "all flesh" (Joel 2:28, 29); "any man" (John 7:37-39); "you and your children, and to all . . ." (Acts 2:39).

## Is the Baptism Necessary?

For salvation? No, for we are justified by faith. For life and service? Yes! Jesus commanded His disciples not to depart from Jerusalem until they had been filled with the Spirit (Acts 1:4, 5).

To the converts at Ephesus, Paul gave this instruction: "Be filled with the Spirit" (Ephesians 5:18). This is a clear directive. These are more than words of invitation; they are a Biblical command. If you will sincerely search God's Word, you will discover that the baptism in the Holy Spirit is God's plan for a normal Christian experience.

## Why Should I Be Filled With the Spirit?

Several reasons surface immediately. First, Christ promised to send the Comforter. Second, the Bible commands us to be filled. The main feature of the coming of the Spirit is power for service and not regeneration for eternal life. Whenever we read of the Spirit *filling, falling upon, coming upon,* or *resting upon* people, the reference is always related to power for service, and never to the saving work of the Spirit. The main purpose is to enable us to effectively represent Christ to lost men (Acts 1:8).

Your walk in the Spirit-filled life will lead you into several beautiful experiences. Among them you will find: (1) a greater love and understanding of God's Word; (2) a desire to pray and an ability to pray; (3) a desire for holiness and Christlikeness; (4) a holy boldness to witness; (5) a deep love for the brethren; (6) a yearning compassion for the lost; and (7) an overflowing "joy in the Holy Ghost."

Some will point to the failures of Christians who have been baptized in the Spirit. But their failure does not justify disobedience to the Biblical command, "Be filled with the Spirit." I must make my comparisons with God, His word, and His standards.

## How May I Receive?

This is an important question. To imply that we do not need the experience is an insult to God. To be indifferent about God's command to "be filled with the Spirit" is no less an insult. But the experience is not earned or merited. As salvation, healing, and the gifts of the Holy Spirit are not earned, so the baptism in the Holy Spirit comes by grace and faith. Further, let it always be remembered that the Baptism is not a proof of spiritual achievement.

While the Bible has much to say about the Baptism, it has little to say as to how we may receive the experience. The work of baptizing believers is God's work. The emphasis of Scripture is not on how we should receive, but on how God will give.

We gain most of our instruction by observing what the disciples were told to do. They were told to tarry, literally to "sit down," and to remain there for a purpose. They "all continued with one accord in prayer and supplication" (Acts 1:14).

Peter exhorted his questioners to "repent" (2:38). Known sin must be confessed. God gives the Holy Spirit "to them that obey him" (5:32). Associated with repentance is faith. Faith is the condition on which God bestows all His gifts.

The Lord has promised to fill those who hunger and thirst after Him (Matthew 5:6). We are to ask with intense desire (Luke 11:13; Jeremiah 29:13; Acts 1:14). Continual praise opens our hearts to receive and opens heaven's gates (Psalm 100:4; Luke 24:53).

If you think that you don't need the Baptism, that you can do quite well without the experience, you will not receive. You must *ask* to receive and *seek* to find. Jesus promised the Holy Spirit "to them that ask him" (Luke 11:13).

Finally, you are urged to "take." Revelation 22:17 states: "And whosoever will, let him take the water of life freely." This word *take* is the word translated "receive" in the passages related to receiving the Spirit. Focus on God, repent, obey, believe, hunger, thirst, and take.

Keep three scriptural principles in mind about the baptism in the Holy Spirit:

1. *A great purpose*—"Ye shall receive power . . . ye shall be witnesses" (Acts 1:8).

2. *A comprehensive power*—"The promise is unto you . . . your children . . . all that are afar off . . ." (2:39).

3. *A clear challenge*—"Have ye received . . . since ye believed?" (19:2).

# 6
## The Evidence

*Read:* Acts 2:1-4; 1 Corinthians 12:1-11; Ephesians 5:18-20. *Key Verse:* "And they were all filled with the Holy Ghost, and began to speak with other tongues, as the Spirit gave them utterance" (Acts 2:4). (See statement #8 on p. 127.)

In the previous chapter we gave consideration to the baptism in the Holy Spirit. We found that the Bible teaches that the experience is for all believers, and that it is not an option or luxury. God commands us to be filled with the Spirit. We also looked at the answer to the question, "How may I receive?"

Now another important question surfaces. How can you know that you have been baptized in the Holy Spirit? There must be some evidence of the promised Gift, or how else will you know that you have received this Baptism?

Let's settle on some basic assumptions. The evidence must be a Biblical sign. Further, the sign should be recognizable by both the receiver and others nearby.

A definite scriptural foundation for the evidence must be established. Speaking in tongues was prophesied by Isaiah some 700 years before the Day of Pentecost (Isaiah 28:11, 12). That this refers to the supernatural experience of other tongues is beyond contradiction, for Paul in his treatment of the subject links Isaiah's prophecy directly with the New Testament experience (1 Corinthians 14:

53

21). Jesus himself foretold: "They shall speak with new tongues" (Mark 16:17).

## Why the Book of Acts?

Where would we logically look for this evidence? In the New Testament? in the Gospels? True, there is much in the Gospels about the promise of the Father, but the Spirit was not yet given (John 7:39).

The Epistles? The Epistles were written to churches whose members had received the baptism in the Holy Spirit. Since the normal experience for Christians in the Apostolic Church included the Baptism, there is no instruction to receive given in the Epistles. Instead the command is given to be filled and to continue to be filled. The wide range of teaching on the Holy Spirit in the Epistles is for the most part of a doctrinal nature.

For the scriptural record of people being baptized in the Holy Spirit we must go to the Book of Acts. The book *Pentecostal Truth* by Myer Pearlman and Frank M. Boyd expresses it very well.[1]

In the Gospels we read of the Spirit in promise; in the Epistles we discover His subjective work in sanctification and His operations in the Church; but in the Acts His *dynamic objective* work in the early history of the Church. Here we shall find the evidence we seek.

As the doctrinal statement of the Assemblies of God states, the baptism in the Holy Spirit is "witnessed by the initial physical sign of speaking with other tongues as the Spirit of God gives them utterance."

## Wind . . . Fire . . . Tongues

The record in the Scriptures is very clear. The experience of the 120 on the Day of Pentecost produced extraordinary effects that were visible to onlookers. Three are cited: utterances in languages never learned by the 120, "a sound from heaven as of a rushing mighty wind," and "cloven tongues like as of fire" (Acts 2:1-4).

We believe that the initial physical sign is speaking in tongues. But what about the wind and the fire? Should not these signs also accompany a normal Biblical experience of the Spirit's infilling? The wind and the fire were pre-Pentecost phenomena. Speaking in tongues was a distinctly Pentecost and post-Pentecost experience. The wind and the fire were never repeated. Speaking in tongues was the common experience in the recorded instances of the Spirit's outpouring.

In the three instances in the Book of Acts where the phenomenon is recorded, speaking with tongues was the immediate result of a spiritual experience of being filled with the Spirit (2:4; 10:44-47; 19:6). Yes, at Caesarea and Ephesus those who were filled also prophesied, but they first spoke in tongues.

## Five Witnesses

Altogether there are five instances of the outpouring of the Spirit recorded in the Book of Acts. Three are described in detail, one in part, and the other only inferred. From this record we get our understanding of what happened when believers were baptized in the Holy Spirit in the Apostolic Church. In every case where the details are given of people being filled with the Spirit, speaking in tongues is always mentioned.

## Where It All Began

The first and fullest account is of the Day of Pentecost. Here 120 praying disciples were gathered in response to Christ's instruction "to wait for the promise of the Father." With no preconceived notions or prejudices, they surely had no idea what would happen. But suddenly "they were *all* filled with the Holy Ghost, and began to speak with other tongues, as the Spirit gave them utterance" (2:4).

The outstanding supernatural manifestation of the Spirit in the Upper Room was, without controversy, speaking with other tongues. All were filled and *all* spoke in tongues. The fact that God chose tongues as the sign in this initial outpouring of the Spirit carries great significance for all future occasions. Peter recognized that the Day of Pentecost had set an accepted precedent (11:15).

## What Happened in Samaria?

The next account of the outpouring of the Spirit is in Samaria (8:14-18). In this instance there is no indication as to the precise nature of the manifestation given. Simon's keen observation and amazing request prove beyond doubt that there was spectacular evidence, even though tongues are not mentioned.

Peter's rebuke to Simon hints that there was speaking in tongues. He said: "Thou hast neither part nor lot in this matter" (v. 21). The Greek word translated "matter" can also be translated "word," "utterance," or "supernatural utterance." Adam Clarke and Matthew Henry are two among many commentators and scholars who state that the Samaritans spoke with tongues as they received the Holy Spirit.

## The Straight Street Experience

The third account of the reception of the fullness of the Spirit is that of Paul (9:17). The Bible neither states that Paul did nor did not speak with tongues on this occasion. But of one thing we are certain and that is that he did speak with tongues. His strong personal testimony was: "I thank my God, I speak with tongues more than ye all" (1 Corinthians 14:18).

If Paul did not begin to speak with tongues when he was filled, when did he begin? There is every reason to believe that he spoke with tongues at the same point that the other apostles first did—when baptized in the Holy Spirit.

## A Preacher's Delight

For the fourth Biblical record we go to Acts 10:44-47. Under the ministry of Peter, the Gentiles of Cornelius' house were saved and filled with the Holy Spirit. While Peter was preaching, "the Holy Ghost fell on all them which heard the word." How did Peter know? "For they heard them speak with tongues, and magnify God." The evidence that satisfied the surprised and prejudiced Jewish Christians that these Gentiles had been filled with the Spirit was the speaking with tongues. This only goes to prove the unique place this sign was given in the Church.

## After Twenty-three Years

The final account records the experience at Ephesus (Acts 19). Here again the initial evidence was: "They spake with tongues, and prophesied" (v. 6). The record is clear and plain; 23 years after the Day of Pentecost the same identical initial evidence accompanied the gift of the Holy Spirit. Prophesying and magnifying God at Cornelius' house are mentioned here, but speaking in tongues is the common authenticating evidence.

The cumulative testimony of the instances recorded in the Book of Acts where the gift of the Spirit was received, bears out the fact of the continuing evidence as at the Day of Pentecost. The logical conclusion of Acts 10:46 ("For they heard them speak with tongues"), and Peter's report of the incident to the leaders in Jerusalem ("And as I began to speak, the Holy Ghost fell on them, as on us at the beginning" [11:15]), indicate that the Apostolic Church associated speaking with tongues with the baptism in the Holy Spirit.

## Not Most Important

Let it be clearly understood that speaking with tongues was not, and is not, the most important element of the baptism in the Holy Spirit. But speaking in tongues does provide a positive scriptural proof of the fullness of the Spirit within the believer.

Have you noticed Peter's statement in Acts 11:15? "The Holy Ghost fell on them, as on us at the beginning." The word *beginning* is significant. It sets a pattern; a precedent was established which is a pattern to guide the future. Looking back to that "beginning" we note these matters of precedence:

1. The baptism in the Holy Spirit is for all believers, not only for leaders.

2. Speaking in tongues is the initial, physical evidence.

3. Anointed preaching is the major means of evangelism.

4. The power of the Holy Spirit is given to enable the Church to reach large numbers of people.

5. The experience is not always understood by those outside the Church.

## Do All Speak With Tongues?

The doctrine of tongues as evidence of the infilling of the Spirit is at times questioned on alleged scriptural grounds on the basis of Paul's statement: "Do all speak with tongues?" (1 Corinthians 12:30). By an examination of the context we find that Paul is dealing here with the *gifts* of the Spirit, not the *gift* of the Spirit. To wrest his words out of context is to bring confusion.

The Book of Acts deals with the manifestation of tongues as initial evidence. The utterance was spontaneous and *all* spoke. The first Corinthian letter deals with the gift of tongues which is controllable (14:28) and is to be restricted to "be by two, or at the most by three" (v. 27).

Speaking with tongues when being baptized in the Holy Spirit is the same in essence as the gift of tongues, but different in purpose and use. The phenomenon at Pentecost aroused the question, "What meaneth this?" Interest had been stirred, but it was Peter's sermon, preached in a language understood by all present and recorded in Acts 2, that brought conviction. This resulted in another question, "What shall we do?" (v. 37).

## Initial and Physical

We use two terms—*initial* and *physical*—when speaking of tongues as the evidence of the Baptism. These are not Biblical terms. We use them just for what they are, for purposes of definition.

Other evidences of the infilling of the Spirit are not in the same sense *initial* and *physical*, but they

59

are important. They include an overflowing fullness of the Spirit (John 7:37-39; Acts 4:8); a deepened reverence for God (Acts 2:43; Hebrews 12:28); an intensified consecration to God and dedication to His work (Acts 2:42); and a more active love for Christ, His Word, and the lost (Mark 16:20). These evidences are important! They are indications of the Spirit-filled life.

## Why Tongues?

Why did God choose tongues as the evidence? To answer this question I quote from my book *Spiritual Dynamics:*[2]

Why did God choose tongues as the evidence? Speech is the distinctively characteristic manifestation of human personality. In the whole creative order, it is a uniquely human faculty. Thurneysen underscores it with perception, "The mystery of speech is identical with the mystery of personality, with the image of God in man."

But what's so good about other tongues? Unnecessary . . . ridiculous . . . irrational . . . far out? No, it's Biblical. But why not our own languages? The answer is found in the asking. When I speak English, I'm speaking words that are in my own mind, words that manifest my personality. When I speak in tongues as the Holy Spirit gives utterance, I speak words that are in the mind of the Spirit, words that manifest His personality, words uncensored by my mind, words that are a beautiful self-manifestation of the Spirit.

The two last faculties to be surrendered are man's mind and his tongue. In speaking in an unknown tongue, the mind and the tongue are completely given over to the Spirit. As in water baptism the candidate yields to the baptizer until completely immersed in water, so in the Spirit's baptism the seeker yields to Christ until completely given over to the Spirit.

While there are other evidences of the baptism in the Holy Spirit besides speaking in an unknown tongue, we must admit that this one sign was chosen in divine wisdom. No other evidence so sufficiently and conclusively satisfies the recipient and the witnesses present, as does this as an initial evidence.

I reemphasize the truth that the baptism in the Spirit was the normal experience in the Apostolic Church. All believers are entitled to and should ardently expect and earnestly seek for the "promise of the Father." It is important that all who receive be able to describe the experience, and pointing back to the Day of Pentecost say, "This is that!"

## Living and Walking in the Spirit

The baptism in the Holy Spirit is the beginning of a lifelong experience of great spiritual development. The Spirit comes to abide, not just to visit. Jesus promised the Comforter who would "abide with you forever."

Without the continuing presence of the Spirit, our lives are powerless and fruitless. We are like electric cords—useless unless plugged in. We must maintain our connection to the Source. When we do, we will give evidence of His abiding presence. "If we live in the Spirit, let us also walk in the Spirit" (Galatians 5:25).

## The Supply of the Spirit

The baptism in the Holy Spirit represents divine equipment placed at the disposal of the believer by God. Use this equipment according to God's pattern and you'll have the fruit of the Spirit in your life. Fail to use what God has given and your spiritual life will be barren.

Tucked away in Philippians 1:19 is a beautiful and revealing bit of autobiography: "For I know that this shall turn to my salvation through your prayer, and the supply of the Spirit of Jesus Christ." We lift out five words—"the supply of the Spirit." Some quite appropriately have called this "the plus of the Spirit."

The word translated *supply* relates to the realm of plenty. The term has several interesting meanings and applications. They are worthy of examination.

The supply of the Spirit is more than enough to keep you going. More than one translator takes *supply* to mean "a rich provision." In this sense the word has to do with nutrition. There is ample provision for your sustenance.

Again, the supply of the Spirit is more than enough to help you out. The term alludes to that which undergirds and strengthens. The Spirit intervenes in your extremity. He is a vital addition to your resources.

The supply of the Spirit is more than enough to lead you on. The term carries the hint of coordination. Wuest speaks of "a fully-proportioned supply." He is a needed corrective for your deficiencies.

And the supply of the Spirit is more than enough to see you through. The term was used to describe essential military supplies that enabled an army to go through a long campaign and gain final victory.

Ask yourself the question: Am I living up to the limit of what God makes possible for me in the Holy Spirit? You can have *the plus of the Spirit!*

---

[1] Myer Pearlman and Frank M. Boyd, *Pentecostal Truth* (Springfield, MO: Gospel Publishing House), p. 58.

[2] G. Raymond Carlson, *Spiritual Dynamics* (Springfield, MO: Gospel Publishing House, 1976), pp. 70, 71.

# 7
## Supernatural Enablements

*Read:* 1 Corinthians 12; 13; 14; Romans 12:3-8; Ephesians 4:7-16; 1 Peter 4:10, 11. *Key Verse:* "But the manifestation of the Spirit is given to every man to profit withal" (1 Corinthians 12:7).

While the Statement of Fundamental Truths declares the position of the Movement on the subject of the baptism in the Holy Spirit and the evidence of that experience, there is no comment on the gifts of the Holy Spirit. There is great interest in this vital subject and a brief chapter will be devoted to it.

There are some who accuse us Pentecostals of putting too much emphasis on the gifts of the Holy Spirit. But Paul, by the inspiration of the Spirit, declares that "to each one is given the manifestation of the Spirit for the common good" (1 Corinthians 12:7, *NASB*). What God counts profitable is not for any person to call unprofitable.

### For Profit

The gifts of the Holy Spirit are profitable to the believer and to the entire assembly. They are not a hobby to play with. The gifts are placed in the Church by God himself. They are tools with which to do His work and weapons with which to do battle against the enemy. We have a responsibility to recognize and appreciate these supernatural provisions from our Lord.

63

## Gifts and Fruit

There are nine gifts of the Spirit enumerated in 1 Corinthians 12. The fruit of the Spirit is given in a list of nine qualities of character in Galatians 5. The gifts are the word of wisdom, the word of knowledge, faith, gifts of healing, the working of miracles, prophecy, discerning of spirits, tongues, and interpretation of tongues. The fruit of the Spirit is listed as love, joy, peace, long-suffering, gentleness, goodness, faith, meekness, and temperance.

There is a difference in the two lists. Gifts are functional; fruit is a quality of life. Gifts are bestowed; fruit is growth because of implanting. Gifts are given and are complete; fruit is gradual in development, the result of spiritual growth.

## Supernatural Enablement

Spiritual gifts must never be interpreted as natural endowments. They are supernatural enablings from God. The gifts of healing have nothing to do with medicine or surgery. Speaking in tongues has nothing to do with linguistic ability or the learning of languages. The word of wisdom is not glorified common sense. Prophecy is not merely preaching.

The gifts are gifts of the Spirit. As such, they are resident in the Spirit. They are manifested and not imparted. They are manifested according to the will of God and not according to our merit.

## Some No-No's

Never is the manifestation of a gift to be for the promotion of human popularity and personality. Nor is the manifestation of a gift to be an indication of supposed spirituality. And neither are the gifts to be employed for excessive emotional enjoyment.

The New Testament Church did not depend on the gifts of inspired utterance for matters of church government (Acts 6:1-7; 1 Timothy 3:1-13). Doctrine was not established by these gifts (Acts 15). Guidance is not to be sought through the prophetic gift, although it may be a confirmation of God's callings (Galatians 2:1, 2). Utterance gifts are not to be used for interpreting Scripture, for the utterances are themselves to be judged (1 Corinthians 14:29).

## There Is Always a Purpose

The manifestation of spiritual gifts in the church is scriptural and accomplishes God's purpose. When they are scripturally patterned, they fulfill the need for supernatural ministry in and to the body of Christ. "In each of us the Spirit is manifested in one particular way, for some useful purpose" (1 Corinthians 12:7, *NEB*).

Gifts are not an absolute possession. The Lord is the administrator and gifts are in the Spirit who indwells the believer. The consistent manifestation of a gift demands a consistent contact with the Giver. God wills that we are to be filled with the Holy Spirit. When we are, we have the potential to be used by God to minister to any need that may arise in the church. Only as the Holy Spirit supplies the gift at a particular moment for a particular situation will the ministry of a member of the Body be effective.

## Where Do You Fit In?

Each of us as members of the body of Christ has a place and function assigned us by the will of God (1 Corinthians 12:27, 28; Ephesians 4:11, 16). These we term *ministries*. They range from the four major ministries of *apostle, prophet, evangelist,* and *pastor-teacher* (Ephesians 4:11) to *ministry, exhortation, giving, ruling, showing mercy* (Romans 12:3-8), *helps,* and *governments* (1 Corinthians 12:28).

Different gifts will be needed by a "ministry" on different occasions. The power and sovereignty of the Holy Spirit is there to supply the "gift" as it is needed. He may use any Spirit-filled Christian at any time. We are to be ready for the Spirit to use us in ministry by whatever gift He may choose.

In all cases the gifts of the Spirit are mentioned by Paul in a context that emphasizes the unity and edification of the Church as a whole. But the emphasis on the great variety of the gifts is almost as strong as the emphasis on the purpose of unity. Yet this variety always functions within the unity of the Body. The unity is first and fundamental; the variety is second and subsequent. The gift is to be used "for the common good" (1 Corinthians 12:7, *NASB*).

### Do You Know the "Regs"?

First Corinthians calls for these regulations:

1. *Motivation*—love (chapter 13).

2. *Maturity*—"Be not children in understanding: . . . be men" (14:20).

3. *Edification*—called for seven times (vv. 3, 4, 5, 12, 17, 26). All is to edify, to build up, to add to, to contribute to the common good.

4. *Order*—all is to be "done decently and in order" (vv. 33, 40).

The exercise of an utterance gift can be judged (v. 29) by asking these questions:

1. Does it agree with the Word of God?

2. Does it glorify the Lord Jesus?
3. Does it witness with your own spirit?
4. Is it ministered in love?
5. Can it stand the test of being judged by others?

Further guidelines are given in the following Scripture passages:

1. *Forbid not* (1 Corinthians 14:39).
2. *Desire earnestly* (12:31; 14:1, 39)
3. *Evaluate* (14:26-33)
4. *Despise not* (1 Thessalonians 5:20)
5. *Prove* (v. 21).
6. *Hold fast* (v. 21).
7. *Neglect not* (1 Timothy 4:14)
8. *Stir up* (2 Timothy 1:6).
9. *Take heed* [*to fulfill*] (Colossians 4:17).

We need to beware lest we be educated away from the idea that we need the full power of the Holy Spirit. Our dependence must not rest upon organization, man, power, or publicity. We must never dogmatize into mere terminology this simple and yet intensely profound experience of the baptism in the Holy Spirit and His supernatural enablements.

### Gifts of Revelation—Power to Know Supernaturally

The first gift is the *word of wisdom.* This is supernatural wisdom given by inspiration of the Spirit. Through this gift a person is divinely enabled to speak the right word for help or direction in a given situation.

The apostles exercised this gift at the crisis hour when there was murmuring about the unequal distribution of funds. They called for the church to choose deacons so that they (the apostles) could give themselves continually "to prayer, and to the ministry of the word." (Acts 6:4). James apparently exercised this gift during another crisis (15:13-18). The word of wisdom is not diplomacy, tact, human skill, glorified intelligence, or psychology. No amount of experience develops this wisdom; it is supernatural.

The second gift is the *word of knowledge*. This is a divine communication by revelation of facts, relating to earth, that are not known. The knowledge communicated through this gift is not received through scholarly achievement. It neither makes a scholar, nor can it be attained by study, education, mental ability, or experience. Paul was given knowledge while in a storm at sea (27:10).

The next gift in this category is *discerning of spirits*. This is the ability to recognize evil spirits which cause wrong physical or spiritual conditions. The manifestation comes not by the keen insight of the psychiatrist, human shrewdness, or the ability to read character. It has nothing to do with ESP, nor is it related to a spirit of judging or carping criticism. It is knowing and judging, but never guessing.

Through this gift Peter exposed Ananias and Sapphira (5:1-11) and Simon the sorcerer (8:23). Paul discerned that Elymas was a child of the devil (13:6-12) and unmasked the demon spirit in the fortune-teller at Philippi (16:16-18).

### Gifts of Power—Power to Act Supernaturally

*Faith* as a gift enables a believer to exercise faith, beyond saving faith, for victories in the cause of Christ. It is special faith, miraculous faith, mountain-moving faith (Mark 11:23). Dorcas was undoubtedly raised from the dead through the gift of faith and that, in turn, was the working of a miracle (Acts 9:36-42). Faith ends and miracles and healings begin.

*Gifts of healing* is the supernatural enduement of power whereby physical healing is ministered to the sick. Gifts of healing do not make you a healer; healing rests with the sovereignty of God. This gift was common in the ministry of Christ and the apostles. It is in exercise today to which thousands give testimony.

The *working of miracles* is an event occurring in the physical world which is contrary to nature and resulting from a supernatural intervention or an interruption of the system of nature as we know it. This gift is present in some healings, especially where divine creative power is present. The restoration of a destroyed or removed organ is an example.

But miracles include more than bodily cures, though none are specifically spelled out in the Book of Acts or the Epistles. An example of the gift is recorded in Acts 19:11, 12 as "miracles by the hands of Paul." Then, of course, Acts 9:36-42 records the raising to life of Dorcas, and Acts 20:9, 10 the restoring to life of Eutychus.


## Gifts of Inspiration—Power to Speak Supernaturally

The *gift of tongues* is a divinely given ability to speak in other languages, expressing words one has never learned, but which are directly communicated by the Holy Spirit. The gift is for private prayer and worship. When accompanied by its sister gift of interpretation, the church is edified.

*Interpretation of tongues* is an inspired explanation in commonly understood language of an inspired utterance in an unknown language. The gift of tongues and the gift of interpretation of tongues are unique to the New Testament, occurring after Pentecost.

69

*Prophecy* is unpremeditated utterance in one's own language. It is a supernatural manifestation given for edification, exhortation, and comfort.

## Perfect Balance

Paul told Timothy: "God has not given us the spirit of fear; but of power, and of love, and of a sound mind" (2 Timothy 1:7). In 1 Corinthians 12 we have the power; in chapter 13 we have the love; and in chapter 14 we have the sound mind, the mind of perfect balance. The last verse of 1 Corinthians 12 exhorts us to "covet earnestly the best *gifts*" and give them to *love* for control. The first verse of chapter 14 says get *love* and give it the *gifts* for its task.

# 8
## Sanctification

*Read:* 1 Corinthians 6:11; Hebrews 10:10, 14; 1 Thessalonians 5:23, 24; John 15:3; 17:17; Ephesians 5:26; Romans 6:9-13; Galatians 5:16, 17; 1 John 2:1, 6. *Key Verse:* "I beseech you therefore, brethren, by the mercies of God, that ye present your bodies a living sacrifice, holy, acceptable unto God, which is your reasonable service" (Romans 12:1). (See statement #9 on p. 127.)

### Not One but Three

You are not one person, but three—the one *you* see yourself to be, the one *other people* see you to be, and the one *God* knows you to be. Sanctification is the means by which God brings you to be what He *wants* you to be.

Sanctification is the grand moral purpose of God for His people. In the study of the doctrine of sanctification, we reach the experimental side of salvation.

Justification—the great doctrine of the Reformation—means a change in my standing before God. Regeneration means a change in my nature. Sanctification means a change in my character and conduct. Sanctification touches immediately my life and testimony.

Justification has to do with God's provision for a change in my position. Sanctification has to do with God's provision for a change in my condition. Justifi-

71

cation, redemption, and regeneration deal with the pardon of my sin. Sanctification deals with deliverance from sin's power.

### Dismayed?

Can you have complete victory over sin? The answer is in understanding what Christ did for you at Calvary. You can appropriate His provision and find deliverance from the frustration and defeat of sin's dominion. Liberty and victory in Christ are available for you. By identification with Christ you can find deliverance from bondage.

In justification God declares the sinner righteous. In sanctification God makes the sinner righteous.

What do the terms *justification* and *sanctification* mean? *Justification* is the judicial act of God by which He pronounces the believing sinner righteous, freeing him from condemnation, and restoring him to divine favor (Romans 3:24).

### Sanctified . . . Separated . . . Set Apart

The word *sanctify* comes from the same root as holy, holiness, hallow, consecrate, and saint. The process of sanctification involves: (1) a cleansing from defilement, and (2) a conformity to the likeness of God.

Sanctification involves two great truths. The first is *consecration* or a *true relationship* to God. The root idea of the terms *holy* and *sanctify* is separation. The Bible speaks of persons and places being sanctified or holy. This means that such were separated in the sense of being set apart from others for God's possession. To illustrate—the 7th day was set apart (Genesis 2:3); a house or a field could be sanctified (Leviticus 27:14-16); and the Levites were separated (Numbers 8:14). The root idea is consecration. We are redeemed in order to be set apart.

The second truth involved in sanctification is *purification* or a *true condition* before God. The presence of God by the Holy Spirit in our hearts and lives will purify our thought life, bringing all our motives and desires into subjection to God's will (2 Timothy 2:21; 1 John 1:7).

### Restoring the Original

A patron of the arts was browsing through a secondhand store. Suddenly his heart picked up its beat. Before him was a painting that most people would have considered worthless. But his expert eye detected another painting underneath. Knowing that many a masterpiece had been concealed in just that way, he casually bought the picture. At home he began the painstaking job of restoring the original painting. After hours of "tender, loving care," a masterpiece was restored to its original beauty.

Of all God's creation, man was the masterpiece. Degraded and defaced with sin and shame and covered with evil, he wasn't recognizable as the great masterpiece of Creation. But a purchase price was paid at Calvary. Our soiled and ruined lives were bought with the precious Blood. When we believed, we were justified (Romans 1:17; 5:1). That was redemption and justification.

Sanctification is God's continuing process of restoring us; recreating in us the beauty He originally planned. The work will be complete when our redemption is complete and we receive glorified bodies.

To redeem man God had to do two things. First, He must justify the sinner and bestow on him the gift of righteousness, so He can accept him into His holy presence. Second, He must sanctify that same sinner so that he will be holy. He must declare the sinner righteous and then make the sinner righteous.

We have said all this to point out the value of sanctification and holiness. There are some who believe in "justification by faith," but would be content to live in carnality and sin. God calls us to holiness. We are urged to "cleanse ourselves from all filthiness of the flesh and spirit, perfecting holiness in the fear of God" (2 Corinthians 7:1). God wants a holy people: "For God hath not called us unto uncleanness, but unto holiness" (1 Thessalonians 4:7). "But as he which hath called you is holy, so be ye holy . . . because it is written, Be ye holy; for I am holy" (1 Peter 1:15, 16).

### Believe and Behave

Believe and behave! These are the responsibilities of a Christian. The first brings a man into fellowship with God; the latter gives evidence that he has fellowship with God. When we believe we enter the *straight gate*. When we behave we walk in the *narrow way*. According to Billy Graham: "A Christian ought to live so that he'd not be afraid to sell the family parrot to the town gossip!"

The work of sanctification by the Holy Spirit begins in us at the time of our conversion. If we claim to be "justified" or "forgiven" and "accepted" of God, we ought to begin to produce evidence. How can we "continue in sin" (Romans 6:1)?

### Income Tax Return Okay?

"Sanctification is just taking justification seriously," is the way one theologian puts it. How seriously do you take your standards of conduct as a justified, converted person? Does your income tax return bear up under the scrutiny of God? What about your conversations? your business dealings?

I believe that basically almost everyone really wants to be good. The Bible tells us about a man who wanted to be good and do good, but struggle and failure overcame him. Listen to his agonizing confession:

> I don't understand myself at all, for I really want to do what is right, but I can't. I do what I don't want to—what I hate. I know perfectly well that what I am doing is wrong, and my bad conscience proves that I agree with these laws I am breaking. But I can't help myself. . . . It is sin inside me that is stronger than I am. . . .
>
> I know I am rotten through and through. . . . No matter which way I turn I can't make myself do right. I want to but I can't. When I want to do good, I don't; and when I try not to do wrong, I do it anyway. Now if I am doing what I don't want to, it is plain where the trouble is: sin still has me in its evil grasp (Romans 7:15-20, *The Living Bible*).

## Isn't There Any Help?

This man, Paul, then asks: "Who will free me from my slavery to this deadly lower nature?" And he answers the question with joy and triumph: "Thank God! It has been done by Jesus Christ our Lord. He has set me free" (vv. 24, 25).

The gospel guarantees the *means* by which forgiveness of our sins is made possible, and it provides the *means* by which we can be liberated from the power of sin. When God declared me righteous in His eyes, His action was not isolated from His other actions that will ultimately make me conform to His image.

How, then, can we find this place of victory over

sin and conformity to the divine image? The answer—it's all in Christ and His provision (1 Corinthians 1:30). Christ is made to be:

1. Our *righteousness*, which has to do with our justification (2 Corinthians 5:21).

2. Our *sanctification*, which has to do with our being conformed to the image of God (Ephesians 3:16, 17; 1 Thessalonians 5:23; Romans 12:1, 2).

3. Our *redemption*, which, in this instance, we mean to be the "redemption of our body" (Romans 8:23). This will be the final act in God's great redemptive plan. His ultimate purpose will be fulfilled as the redeemed "shall be like him; [when they] see him as he is" (1 John 3:2), "conformed to the image of his Son" (Romans 8:29). Planned by the Father, provided by the Son, and applied by the Holy Spirit. What grandeur, glory, and grace!

## The Purpose of the Father

Sanctification is in the purpose of God: "For this is the will of God, even your sanctification" (1 Thessalonians 4:3). God's will indicates two things: (1) His determination, and (2) His desire and delight. The sanctification of the believer is God's desire and delight. His will is frustrated by our waywardness.

## The Purchase of the Son

The Bible states that "we are sanctified through the offering of the body of Jesus Christ" (Hebrews 10:10). Christ not only died for our sins to reconcile us to God, but He arose that we might have, by His life, His image restored in our character.

The New Testament gives only one formula for sanctification. It is found in Romans 6. It's a matter of appropriating by faith and identifying ourselves

76

with Christ. Three terms used in the chapter will help us:

1. *Knowing.* "Knowing this, that our old man is crucified with him, that the body of sin might be destroyed, that henceforth we should not serve sin" (v. 6). This is the fact of God's Word. We are commanded to take our stand on this truth. The first step in appropriating is *knowing*.

2. *Reckoning.* "Likewise reckon ye also yourselves to be dead indeed unto sin, but alive unto God through Jesus Christ our Lord" (v. 11). The term *reckon* applies to mathematics and means "to count, compute, to take into account."

We are to reckon two things: (1) that the old man has died and the sinful nature has been rendered powerless; and (2) that we "are alive unto God"— new life has been imparted to us. Our reckoning is by faith, not based on emotions. The Cross separates us from the authority of sin. We have new hearts and are under new management. Occupy your mind with Christ's provision for you. Reckon on it.

3. *Yielding.* "Neither yield ye your members . . . unto sin: but yield yourselves unto God . . ." (v. 13). You put into actual practice the exhortation to reckon yourself dead unto sin and alive unto God by doing something that is a work of faith. *Your will is the steering gear of your soul.* You are a free moral agent, but you were created to be mastered by God, not Satan. The unsaved man sins because he is driven to do so. The Christian sins because he consents with his will to yield to temptation.

Sanctification is not eradication of the old nature, nor is it supression—struggling internally to maintain outward composure. Sin is not dead, but the Christian can be dead to sin.

## By the Power of the Spirit

Sanctification is the operation of the law of life over the law of sin and death (Romans 8:1, 2). Faith as a definite act receives Christ for justification. Faith as a constant attitude appropriates Christ for sanctification. The Holy Spirit assures us of the former and effects in us the latter.

Through union with the risen and glorified Saviour, a new power, the Holy Spirit, enters human nature to subdue sin. Through the Spirit, the righteousness that the Law required is fulfilled in us (not by us). We walk in the Spirit and He brings us into a life of victory in Christ.

The Spirit-controlled life is shown in Romans 8 to be marked by: (1) spiritual harmony—"life and peace" (v. 6); (2) spiritual victory—"body is dead . . . but the Spirit is life" (v. 10); (3) spiritual mastery—"led by the Spirit" (v. 14); and (4) spiritual certainty—(vv. 15-39).

## By the Pages of the Scriptures

The Bible teaches us that we "are clean through the Word" (John 15:3) and sanctified through the truth which is God's Word (17:17). We are made holy, not by the paper, ink, and leather of the Book, but by the literal Word, the great instrument which the Spirit uses.

Christ sanctifies and cleanses the Church "with the washing of water by the word" (Ephesians 5:26, 27). As believers, we have experienced the washing of regeneration (Titus 3:5). But there must be a daily washing of the defilements and imperfections as they are revealed by the Word, which is like a mirror (James 1:21-25).

We can't expect God to keep us in holiness if we

deliberately and knowingly place ourselves in situations that make it impossible. Obedience to His will, as revealed in His Word, will keep us out of such situations.

## Instantaneous and Progressive

When we believe on Christ as Saviour, we become saints (literally, "sanctified ones"). In this sense, sanctification is instantaneous as acknowledged in 1 Corinthians 1:1, 2 and 6:11. But sanctification is also progressive. God has imputed His holiness to us, but we must make that holiness actual in everyday life.

Sanctification must be understood as progress in refining and enriching the soul, and not as a slow process of deliverance from some known sin. As we live and walk by the help and guidance given us by the Spirit and the Word, we enjoy Christian growth and progress toward the day when we shall stand in Him perfect and complete, all aglow with the very likeness of the glorious Son of God.

## Chipping Here to Fit There

A Christian stopped to watch a stone mason working at a church construction site. "What are you doing?" he asked the mason who was chipping a small stone. Pointing to the top of the nearly completed building, the workman replied, "I'm chipping the last stone to fit in way up there."

With a word of thanks the Christian went on his way with a pleasant smile on his face. God had illustrated to him the great truth of trials on earth and glory in heaven—"chipping down here to fit up there."

# 9
## *What About the Church?*

*Read:* 1 Corinthians 3:9-11; 12:12-27; Ephesians 1:22, 23; 2:19-22; 4:11-13; 5:25-32. *Key Verse:* "Christ is the head of the church: and he is the saviour of the body" (Ephesians 5:23). (See statements #10 and #11 on pp. 127, 128.)

### Five Minus Three Equals Two

Five minus three equals two. That's a simple equation in arithmetic. You learned it early in life. But suppose it represents personal tragedy in your life?

A prominent diplomat was called home from his office one day. His son had been fatally injured in an elevator accident. His wife's health had been failing, and now the shock of his death was too great and became fatal. His stepson was removed by blood relatives. With almost one fell swoop the man's family numbered no longer five but two. Five minus three equals two.

Where could such a man turn for help? Friends? Inner resources? Cultism? Throw everything overboard? What did he do? None of these. He came to the conclusion that he must turn to what he termed "the worn comfort of the church." Think about it. He did not say, "The worn-out comfort of the church," but, "The worn comfort." Christ, through His church, provides comfort and strength that has worn well. God has an antidote for loneliness; it's a Christ-created fellowship, life in the Church.

## But What Is the Church?

"Our church is 2 miles from our house." "We are building a new church." "Our church has a tall steeple." In this usage you are speaking of a *building*.

"Our church has 300 members." Now you're talking about a *congregation*. Or, "Were you in church yesterday?" Here you're speaking of a *worship service*. And again you might say, "Our church has its headquarters in Springfield, Missouri. "Church" in this setting connotes an *organized fellowship*.

Another may talk about the Church as being all true believers. This is the true scriptural meaning of the *Church*.

Thus to some the word *church* describes a building; to others a congregation, a denomination, a branch of Christendom, a worship service, or all Christians, as distinguished from Muslims, for instance.

However, the New Testament meaning of the word *church* is limited to two concepts: (1) that of a local assembly meeting to worship God and to bear witness to faith in Christ; and (2) the whole company of believers in Christ, including all generations from Pentecost to the completion of this age.

The word *church* is used over 110 times in the New Testament. This frequency indicates its importance, and this is sufficient reason to have a proper understanding of the scriptural meaning of the word.

## Kuriakos . . . Ekklesia

The English term *church* comes from a Greek

81

word *kuriakos* meaning "that which belongs to the Lord." The Apostolic Church had at its disposal at least half a dozen different terms that could have been used. The Holy Spirit chose, however, to use the Greek word *ekklesia,* a term that apparently was not used by any major religious groups of that day. The word means an assembly of called-out ones or maybe more specifically "to call together." There are two emphases—a group of people called unto the Lord and then unto one another.

## There Is a Difference

There is a difference between *the* Church and *a* church. The first is the Christian Church and the second is an institutional church. The former is the entire Body of true believers, those now living and those at home with the Lord. The institutional church is made up of persons who are corporately organized and subscribe to beliefs and practices as required for membership.

Christ established the Christian Church. The institutional church is the result of man's understanding of the will of God to find expression for the Christian Church. The institutional church and the Christian Church should be in perfect agreement, but at times they are not. They may even be in conflict.

The Church is an organism. There must, however, be organization to give direction and force to the organism. This is the linking of divine and human forces to form a partnership to fulfill the purpose of God. The New Testament has much to say about the local assembly—its mission, ministry, officers, membership, support, standards, and discipline.

## Creaking Machinery

Today far too much emphasis is placed on the human side of the Church. Organization followed the welding together of the 120 at Pentecost into a new organic community. An organism is basic, but organization is also a necessary part.

Never forget that the Church is divine, not human. It is the creation of God and not of men. Our efforts don't make the Church. We receive and are received into the Church by divine action through the new birth.

We are prone to think and speak in terms of *churches*, and that's okay as long as we differentiate between the Church and churches. In God's sight there is only one Church: "The church of God, which he hath purchased with his own blood" (Acts 20:28). Jesus promised: "I will build my church; and the gates of hell shall not prevail against it" (Matthew 16:18). He kept His promise, building the one and only true Church—His church.

Through the centuries church bodies have arisen—the Roman Catholic Church, the Greek Orthodox Church, the Protestant churches. Christ built something more scriptural, more enduring, and more comprehensive.

## Bricks . . . Plaster . . . Lumber . . . Concrete

Christ's church is bought with *blood*, not built with bricks.

The Church consists of *people* and not of plaster.

The Church is enclosed with *love* and not with lumber.

The Church finds its strength in *consecration* and not in concrete.

The New Testament employs at least three significant symbols of the Christian Church—a *body*, a *building*, and a *bride*. All three are found in the Epistle to the Ephesians. The metaphor of the body suggests *life* (1:22, 23). The building (2:20-22) suggests an *Indweller*. The analogy of the bride (5:25-32) suggests a relationship demanding *love*.

## The Body and Its Head

The Church is Christ's body and He is the Head. The similarity between functions of the human body and Christ's church is developed in detail in 1 Corinthians 12. The analogy provides the basis for some very practical exhortations in Romans 12:4-21.

Just as a body with several heads would be a monstrosity, a head with many bodies would be likewise. There is one Body to which all true believers, regardless of local church affiliation, belong. The Church is not a hierarchical organization to which you are admitted by a mechanical rite. The Church is not held together by a complex structure of rituals and administered with pomp.

## Seven Vital Principles

Seven principles vividly picture the proper functioning of Christ's body in 1 Corinthians 12:12-27:

1. *The principle of interdependence*—" . . . not one member, but many." Each part is for the other. The foot walks for the body; the eye sees for the body; the hand grasps for the body.

2. *The principle of appreciation*—"The eye cannot say unto the hand, I have no need of thee. . . ." Every member has his place. You may be only an "eyelash" and yet you are needed. We must appreciate you for your part in His body.

3. *The principle of diversity*—"If the whole body

84

were an eye, where were the hearing?" God made each of us different. Let's not be critical of our brothers and sisters. In the will of God we are diverse. God uses that variety.

4. *The principle of recompense*—"Our uncomely parts have more abundant comeliness." The weaker members of our physical bodies receive more attention and that is true in Christ's body.

5. *The principle of divine choice*—"God hath set the members . . . in the body, as it hath pleased him." God is making us to be what He wants us to be.

6. *The principle of yielding*—"Because I am not the eye, I am not of the body. . . . If the whole body were an eye, where were the hearing?" Be what you are. Content yourself. I can't be or do what others do, but I can be and do what God wants me to be and do.

7. *The principle of ministry*—" . . . no schism. . . . Care one for another. . . . One member suffers, all the members suffer . . . one . . . honored, all the members rejoice." Each of us contributes to the others. A healthy member will function within its limits and at the direction of the head in the physical body. May we respond in like manner in Christ's body.

## The Building and Its Cornerstone

A contractor who built the house in which he lives can look on his completed work with the pride of ownership. He can say: "This is my house, I planned it, built it, and paid for it. From the blueprint to the day of 'open house,' I gave my full attention to its completion."

In a much greater sense, God can say: "This Church, this Building, this Temple is mine. I planned it. I purchased it through the death of my

Son. It is my 'habitation . . . through the Spirit'" (Ephesians 2:22).

The *foundation* is upon the apostles and prophets. This does not imply apostolic succession, but rather being based on the writings of the apostles and prophets—the Scriptures.

The *cornerstone* is Christ. This is developed in 1 Peter 2:4-10; 1 Corinthians 3:10-16; and Ephesians 2:19-22. The figure suggests three ideas. As the Head of the corner it is Christ who binds the Church together. It is He on whom the Church rests. And He has the place of greatest honor.

We rest on Christ. To find out if a person is a member of the Church, you can ask, "On what are you resting your trust for life and eternity?" Christ is the solid Rock.

A preacher was conducting an open-air meeting in Ireland about the time of the shamrock races. A heckler kept asking him, "Say, mister, what do you know about the shamrock?" After several interruptions, the preacher stopped, looked the heckler in the eye, and replied, "On Christ the solid Rock I stand—all other ground is *sham-rock.*"

The *stones* of which the Building is built are people—converted people. We are "living stones."

The *Inhabitant* of the house is God (1 Corinthians 3:16). He lives in us. And He lives in this Building which has no dividing walls or partitions. We may try to build walls, but God's house has none.


## The Bride and Her Groom

This vivid metaphor is used in Ephesians 5:25-32; Revelation 19:6-21; and 21:1, 2. What a groom is to a bride, that is what—and more—Christ is to the Church.

The life of Christ flows through the Church—it is His body. And the life of the Church is distinct—it is His bride. The Church is never separated from the Bridegroom but at the same time is always distinct from Him.

A bride and groom are not born married. A little girl would often say that when she grew up she was going to marry her brother. He would become embarrassed and reply, "We can't. We're brother and sister, we've grown up together." To which she'd answer, "Yes, but Mommie and Daddy live in the same house and they're married." But her mother and dad weren't born married.

Christ and His bride were originally apart. But now we have become espoused to Him. An espousal, during the time when Christ was on earth, was as sacred as marriage. At present, the Bride is a chaste virgin to be presented to Christ (2 Corinthians 11:1-3).

When the girl of my choice accepted my proposal of marriage, she accepted an engagement ring. That acceptance said that we would have eyes and thoughts for none other. Are you and I true to our heavenly Bridegroom?

## The Purpose of the Church

God had three things in focus when He established the Church:

1. That He might have a people to worship Him in Spirit and truth.
2. That the redeemed might be conformed to the image of His Son.
3. That the world might be evangelized through the power of the Holy Spirit.

# The Ministry

God has provided gifts for the purpose of leading the Church in its threefold mission of (1) ministry to God (worship); (2) ministry to the believer (edification); and (3) ministry to the world (Ephesians 4:11-13).

These ministry gifts are the gifts of Christ to the Church. They are different from the gifts of the Spirit, which are supernatural enablements bestowed on believers. The gifts of Christ are God-appointed ministers to "lead and feed, direct, instruct, and discipline the Church for its own good and development, and for the furtherance of its work for Christ on earth," states P. C. Nelson in *Bible Doctrines*.[1]

The Christian ministry is pastoral, not priestly. A priestly ministry is exercised Godward, while a pastoral ministry is exercised manward. The ministry is "for building up the body of Christ" (Ephesians 4:12, *RSV*), and "to equip God's people for work in his service" (*NEB*).

The "Pastoral Epistles" to Timothy and Titus give us much light on the offices to be held in the local church. The Corinthian Epistles deal with order in the local church.

---

[1] P. C. Nelson, *op. cit.* (1948 edition).

# 10
## *Is Healing for You?*

*Read:* Acts 5:12-16; 10:38; Exodus 15:26; Matthew 8:16, 17; 10:1, 8; Mark 16:17, 18; Isaiah 53:4, 5; 1 Peter 2:24; James 5:14-16. *Key Verse:* "Who his own self bare our sins in his own body on the tree, that we, being dead to sins, should live unto righteousness: by whose stripes ye were healed" (1 Peter 2:24). (See statement #12 on p. 128.)

"Sick? Keep a stiff upper lip. Don't expect God to heal you. Remember Paul's thorn in the flesh." Can that chilling approach be your only hope? Well, that's the way a lot of people think. But that's not God's plan. He made provision for our physical bodies.

### Two Kinds

There are two kinds of healing—natural and supernatural. And, in one sense, all healing is divine. Doctors and medicines would be of little value if it were not for the healing processes put in the human body by God himself. The surgeon's knife and healing remedies serve, where possible, to stop the onslaught of disease. Healing takes place through the materials carried in and by the blood.

Natural healing takes place through this healing process in the body and is often assisted by the use of medicine and surgery. In this sense natural healing is divine because of God's provision in the body and the curative combinations of products taken from the earth created by Him, as well as through the intelligence He has given men.

Supernatural healing, however, is what we normally term *divine healing*. This healing takes place without the aid of medicine or surgeon. This is truly divine healing.

All through the Bible we read of healing for the body. When the Psalmist calls upon all that is within him to bless the Lord for all His benefits, he combines spiritual pardon and physical healing: "Who forgiveth all thine iniquities; who healeth all thy diseases" (Psalm 103:3).

## Casual Readers

Even the most casual reader of the Gospels can't miss the miraculous healings of Jesus. His healing ministry was an outpouring of compassion "to bring healing" to those in need (Luke 9:2, *Amplified*). But beyond that, His miracles and healings were His credentials (7:19-23).

The millennial ministry of Christ will feature a great healing ministry as the "Sun of righteousness arise[s] with healing in his wings" (Malachi 4:2). Then "the inhabitant shall not say, I am sick" (Isaiah 33:24). "Then the eyes of the blind shall be opened, and the ears of the deaf shall be unstopped. Then shall the lame man leap, . . . and the tongue of the dumb sing" (35:5, 6).

## What About Today?

But of vital interest to us, Jesus heals in the 20th century. In the Book of Acts, Luke writes "of all that Jesus began both to do and teach" while He was on earth (1:1). The apostles preached healing and prayed for the sick (3:16). They prayed "that signs and wonders may be done by the name of thy holy child Jesus" (4:29, 30).

## No Proof

If anyone wants to prove that God doesn't heal today, he won't find proof in the Bible. Our Lord said: "These signs shall follow them that believe; . . . they shall lay hands on the sick, and they shall recover" (Mark 16:17, 18). And "Jesus Christ [is] the same yesterday, and today, and for ever" (Hebrews 13:8).

## Reparable

We are forced to acknowledge that since God created us, He certainly is able to repair us. Since He made us, He can and does preserve us. All things are possible with God!

God chose to obligate himself to provide healing for the physical body. This is His gracious provision for His people. He reveals himself: "I am the LORD that healeth thee" (Exodus 15:26). He further obligates himself by saying, "And the LORD will take away from thee all sickness . . ." (Deuteronomy 7:15).

## Which Is Easier?

One day Jesus was busy teaching with several critics skeptically listening. Suddenly a man with palsy was lowered through the roof by four friends. Jesus said to the man: "Thy sins be forgiven thee." Immediately the critics accused Him, under their breath, of being a blasphemer.

To this Jesus said: "Whether is easier, to say, Thy sins be forgiven thee; or to say, Arise, and walk? But that ye may know that the Son of man hath power on

91

earth to forgive sins, (then saith he to the sick of the palsy,) Arise, take up thy bed" (Matthew 9:2-7). And the man was healed, showing that it's as easy for the Lord to heal our bodies as it is for Him to forgive our sins.

Study the ministry of both Jesus and the apostles and you'll find that divine healing was not a peripheral ministry. There is a close connection between the healing ministry of Jesus and His saving, forgiving ministry. If you believe the Bible, you believe the miracles, and you must of necessity recognize the healing power of God.

## Worth Noting

Jesus healed, though doctors were plentiful—there were "many physicians" (Mark 5:26).

Jesus healed, without exception, all who came or were brought to Him (Matthew 8:16; 14:14; 15:30).

Jesus healed all varieties of sicknesses, diseases, deformities, defects, and injuries; including blindness, deafness, paralysis, lameness, withered limbs, fever, palsy, leprosy, epilepsy, lunacy, and even a dismembered ear (4:23, 24; 15:30, 31; 21:14; Luke 22:51). He also delivered people from demons and the problems they caused (Matthew 4:24). And to culminate it all, He raised the dead (Luke 7:12-15; 8:49-55; John 11:43, 44).

Jesus healed chronic cases—12 years (Matthew 9:20); 18 years (Luke 13:11); 38 years (John 5:5).

Jesus healed by a touch, by taking people by the hand, by a command, and by a word. He healed those nearby and those at a distance. The Bible records one that was about 16 miles away (John 4:46-53).

Jesus, in most instances, healed people instantaneously (Matthew 15:30, 31). On occasion He healed gradually (John 4:46-54). In one instance, the Lord indicated that the healing would be in the future (9:7). There is the record of the healing of 10 lepers, without the result being apparent at once (Luke 17:14). As is often the case, the healing of the lepers was dependent on both faith and obedience. In the instance of the blind man at Bethsaida, Jesus took him out of the town, removing him from his surroundings before healing him (Mark 8:22-26).

Jesus transmitted healing power to His followers: to the Twelve (Luke 9:1); to the Seventy (10:1-9); and to believers in general (John 14:12-14).

### After He Left

The Book of Acts is an extension of what Jesus did and taught, not only through the apostles but through a Spirit-filled Church (Acts 1:1, 8; 2:4). We have the reference to the shadow of Peter (5:14, 15) and the handkerchiefs and aprons of Paul (19:11, 12). This latter experience was about 20 years after the Ascension.

Still later, teaching was given regarding the gifts of healing which were manifested in the Church (1 Corinthians 12:9). Over a quarter of a century after the Ascension, James gave instruction on prayer for the sick (James 5:14-16).

### Not Limited

Miracles and healing were not limited to the apostles. The promise of the Lord Jesus was to all believers who would ask in the authority of His name (John 14:12-14). God used the unknown Ananias to bring healing to Saul (Paul) (Acts 9:12-18). Philip, the deacon, was greatly used in a healing ministry (8:5-8).

Church history records the continuing ministry of divine healing. Clement, a contemporary of Paul said, "Men receive the gifts of healing." Over 100 years later Iranaeus stated, "Men healed the sick by laying their hands on them." And still another century later Origen said, "Men had marvelous power in curing, by invoking the divine name, and that of Jesus."

The founder of the Methodist Church believed the words of Luke, the doctor, regarding the Great Physician: "[He] healed them that had need of healing" (Luke 9:11). Wesley testified that the same God who saved his soul healed him of tuberculosis.

In his *Explanatory Notes Upon the New Testament,* Wesley recorded his view on James 5:14.[1] He said: "This single conspicuous gift, which God gave to the church . . . was the whole process of physic in the Christian, till it was lost through unbelief."

The Waldenses, Moravians, Hugenots, Covenanters, Friends, Baptists, and Methodists have all left a record of believing in divine healing and practicing prayer for the sick. The time and era do not matter. God has expressed His will toward us and if we believe His Word, He will fulfill His promise.

## Is There a Basis?

Atonement was and is the basis of healing. It is the basis of every blessing we receive from God. All of the merciful acts of Jesus during His earthly ministry were performed in anticipation of His atoning work at Calvary. When our Lord died on the Cross, He not only bore our sins, but "Himself took our infirmities, and bare our sicknesses" (Matthew 8:17). Isaiah prophesied this 700 years before the birth of Christ.

Matthew did not mention a portion of Isaiah's

prophecy—"with his stripes we are healed"—because it had not yet been fulfilled.

Peter was the one to state the fulfillment of Isaiah 53. He said: "By whose stripes ye were healed" (1 Peter 2:24). He gave testimony of the accomplished work. At Calvary Christ bore our sins and our sicknesses. His ribboned back provided deliverance for our pains, aches, and physical suffering.

Forgiveness of sins now is received in connection with the redemption of our souls. When we are caught up to meet the Lord in the air, we shall receive the redemption of our bodies and shall be changed into His likeness. Divine healing provides a foretaste of this and comes to us through Christ's atoning work.

## How Can I Receive Healing?

First, when sickness comes, *get to God*. The Epistle of James says: "Is any . . . afflicted? let him pray" (5:13). Go to God in private prayer.

## Confess

God's Word teaches us to "confess." This may be the clinic you need. Take personal inventory. Get a release from pride and self-righteousness. "Forgive, and ye shall be forgiven" (Luke 6:37). Search your life to see if there is unconfessed sin that is hindering God's blessing.

## Communion

Further, I believe physical healings should be regular occurrences at the Lord's Table. The benefits of the new covenant which Communion commemorates are twofold: the remission of sins and the healing of physical bodies. I could give many examples of healings I witnessed at Communion services. The Communion service should minister to both soul and body.

## Call for the Elders

The Scriptures clearly teach us to call for help. "Is any sick. . . ? let him call for the elders of the church; . . . let them pray. . . , anointing him with oil in the name of the Lord: and the prayer of faith shall save the sick, and the Lord shall raise him up" (James 5:14, 15). This is the Word of the Lord to His church. You and I need the ministry of Christ's body, His church.

## Gifts of Healings

Gifts of healings are one of the manifestations of the Holy Spirit. But just as the gift of wisdom does not make you wise, gifts of healings will not make you a healer. Like every other gift, this one rests in the sovereignty of God.

There must be some significance to the fact that the word *gifts* is absent from the other eight spiritual gifts in 1 Corinthians 12, and yet it is attached to healing, or literally healings. It appears to indicate that none of us can claim a gift of healing, but rather that God sovereignly empowers an individual with a bestowment of healings, as the occasion demands, to the glory of God. This bestowment does not mean that one so used can heal all cases of sickness.

## The Prayer of Faith

Faith is important. Faith is the hand that reaches out to God and never returns empty.

Who needs the faith for healing? Often the Bible indicates that faith was exercised by the afflicted person (Matthew 9:22, 27-31; Acts 14:9, 10). At other times faith was exercised by sympathetic friends and family members (Matthew 8:13; 15:21-28; Luke 5:20). Often faith was exercised by God's minister (Acts 3:6; 9:36-43). Jesus is no respecter of persons; He is a respecter of faith.

The healings of Jesus came in response to a word of authority. His word, command, or touch was sufficient. This was the basic pattern of the apostolic ministry. May God give us more of this apostolic authority and apostolic results.

## Where's Your Focus?

Whenever the Holy Spirit is moving in the church, healings take place. The ministry of healing can be both misunderstood and exploited. Our place is to avoid polarization, for God is not pleased with either position. Neither misunderstanding nor exploitation should cause us to lessen the scriptural preaching and practice of prayer for the sick.

We need to focus on the source of healing—the Lord Jesus Christ. That's objective. Some may focus subjectively on faith healers. We look to God for divine healing. Let's *teach* God's truth on divine healing. Follow this up with *example*. For you and me to be well taught, but nonpracticing, is not in the will of God. Further, let's *protect* this beautiful truth from abuses. Ministries that are abused bring division.

## How About Doctors?

There is no need to set divine healing in opposition to or in competition with the medical profession.

We are grateful for the skills of physicians which have done so much to alleviate human suffering. We only urge you to try God. First, *call* for God's help. *Call* for the elders of the church. Do that and you're on scriptural ground.

## Not Knowing . . . but Knowing

In humility I acknowledge that I don't understand everything about divine healing. Some receive healing and others do not. At times the answer may be obvious, at other times it is not. My part is to declare God's Word and believe for signs to follow. Healing is in the Great Commission.

This I know—God heals. His Word declares so. Personal experience confirms it. Every member of my family, including my parental family, has experienced divine healing. Some of these healings were of afflictions that did not respond to medical treatment.

Five statements summarize the doctrine of divine healing. It is: (1) the work of God; (2) according to the Word of God; (3) based on the atonement of Christ; (4) in the name of the Lord Jesus Christ; and (5) to the glory of God.

If a need is present and faith is present, the power of the Lord is present too—yes, even today. God is as big as you will believe Him to be!

---

[1]John Wesley, *Explanatory Notes Upon the New Testament* (Naperville, IL: Alec R. Allenson, Inc., 1950 reprint of 1755 ed.).

# 11
## *The Blessed Hope*

*Read:* John 14:1-3; 1 Thessalonians 4:13-18; Matthew 24:21-44; 1 Corinthians 15:51, 52; Luke 21:36; 2 Corinthians 5:10; Titus 2:11-13. *Key Verse:* "Looking for that blessed hope, and the glorious appearing of the great God and our Saviour Jesus Christ" (Titus 2:13). (See statement #13 on p. 128.)

Do you remember the old saying?

> *Twixt optimist and pessimist*
> *The difference is droll;*
> *The optimist sees the doughnut,*
> *The pessimist sees the hole.*

Vast differences of opinion are held by people as they look at today's world. Some have extreme optimism, feeling that the progress of man will lead to an eventual utopia on this earth. Others see only trouble and war, death and destruction, and chaos and crumbling disintegration. To them, all is hopeless.

### Optimist or Pessimist?

The Christian's hope centers in a Person and the sovereignty and final triumph of that Person. For this reason, the Christian is the most optimistic person in the world. He knows that the chaos of today was predicted by our Lord as a forerunner to Christ's second coming. He's aware that God's holy purposes

99

will be fulfilled and Christ will be victorious. Belief in the second advent of our Lord makes us incurable optimists.

## An Explosion Is Coming

Destructive weapons, the selfishness of national interest among the great nations, and the desire "to be" that motivates the evolving nations of the third world—all this only pushes man's fears deeper within himself. The world is not building for peace. Thinking people instinctively sense that we are on the road to an impasse that can only result in a worldwide explosion.

The Bible leaves no doubt about the future. It's not only the revelation of His plan of redemption; it's also the revelation of His plan of the future.

## There Is an Answer

Believe in the "blessed hope" and life with all its changing scenes takes on new meaning. Meaning will come to our tears. We'll better understand the yawning grave that has swallowed the earthly remains of those whom we have lost. They're lost only for a while. A youth is cut down in the morning time of life—a father falls at noonday—a mother is harvested in early afternoon. All seemingly have still so much unrealized potential. Is there an answer? Yes, the "blessed hope" gives the answer.

## No One Lives in a Vacuum

The people who walked on earth in Jesus' day were people like us—"men of like passions." They were tempted and won and sometimes lost. They tried and failed, fought and won. They didn't live in a vacuum apart from pressure. But they were "looking for that blessed hope."

The message of the blessed hope is not a matter for speculation and controversy. The message is a vital part of the gospel. As such it is proclaimed as making the entire Christian message meaningful.

This hope is exclusive to the redeemed in Christ, for the unbeliever is "without hope" (Ephesians 2:12; 1 Thessalonians 4:13). There are two sides to God's dealings with humanity—the *blessing* side and the *judgment* side. Belong to Christ and you'll be on the blessing side. You can look forward to escaping from the impending storm of God's judgment on this world.

## Can We Be Certain?

How can we be certain of this hope? The answer is found in the Bible. About one-fifth of the Bible deals with prophecy. About one-third of all prophecy deals with the second coming of Christ. The Second Coming is referred to eight times as often as Jesus' first coming and twice as often as the Atonement.

William Evans in *The Great Doctrines of the Bible* states that one out of every 30 verses in the Bible deals with the return of Jesus.[1] His return is mentioned 318 times in 216 chapters of the New Testament. The Thessalonian Letters have the Second Coming as their theme. Several New Testament chapters are devoted entirely to this theme (Matthew 24; Mark 13; Luke 21).

The Scripture passages that foretold Christ's first coming were marvelously fulfilled (Psalm 22:16-18; 41:9; 55:12-14; Isaiah 7:14; 9:6; 59:20; Hosea 11:1; Micah 5:2; Zechariah 11:12). The Scripture passages

that prophesy His second coming will likewise be
fulfilled. Let's look at some of those references.

## Christ's Own Promise

You can't read the Bible without observing what
Jesus himself had to say about His coming again. He
made three great promises: (1) "I will build my
church" (Matthew 16:18); (2) I will send my Spirit
(John 15:26); and (3) "I will come again" (14:3). He
kept the first two and He will not fail on the third!

## Angelic Confirmation

As Jesus was ascending into heaven 40 days after
His resurrection, two angels appeared to His disciples and declared: "This same Jesus, which is taken
up from you into heaven, shall so come in like manner as ye have seen him go into heaven" (Acts 1:11).
Note the phrase "in like manner." He'll come in like
manner—in person, suddenly, and to His followers.

## Apostolic Teaching

The apostles are no less emphatic in their teaching
of the Second Coming. I take but four examples:

Paul—"The Lord himself shall descend" (1 Thes-
    salonians 4:16).

John—"When he shall appear" (1 John 3:2; Reve-
    lation 1:7).

Peter—"When the chief Shepherd shall appear"
    (1 Peter 5:4).

James—"The coming of the Lord draweth nigh"
    (James 5:8).

According to Ralph Harris:

The New Testament shows how imminent Jesus'
second coming seemed to the first-century Christians.

In accordance with Paul's instructions, believers commemorated the Lord's death "till he come" (1 Corinthians 11:26). They greeted one another with this reminder [Maranatha, meaning "the Lord cometh," (1 Corinthians 16:22)]. They comforted one another with this hope (1 Thessalonians 4:13-18). Except for the verse of benediction, the very last verse of the New Testament reminds us of His coming and shows the response of a Christian who is prepared, watching, and waiting.[2]

People in both Christian and non-Christian circles lift their heads with interest when the end of the world is discussed. They want to know what it will be like and what their personal destiny will be. Right in the middle of their discussions are references to an event called "the Rapture."

## Rapture? What's That?

It's a non-Biblical word used to describe a thoroughly Biblical event—the catching away of believers to meet the Lord in the air prior to the beginning of the Great Tribulation that will constitute the final 7 years before Christ comes in His revelation.

You won't find the word *rapture* in your Bible, but you will find the phrase "caught up together." That phrase is the source of our word *rapture*. When it was translated into Latin, the root word *raptus* was used, meaning "lifted as by a supernatural force and carried up or away."

The translation of God's people—the first stage of the Second Coming—is called the *Rapture*. The second stage is called the *Revelation*.

The *Rapture* will be a private manifestation in the air to the Church. The *Revelation* will be a public manifestation on the earth: "Every eye shall see him, and they also which pierced him" (Revelation 1:7).

## For and With

In the first stage, the Lord will come in the clouds *for* His church. This will be a display of love and grace. In the second, He will come to earth *with* His church. This will bring a display of His righteous anger toward a rebellious earth (2 Thessalonians 1:7, 8).

## A Divine Airlift

The coming of Christ for His church will be a divine airlift. Three things will take place:

1. The Lord himself shall descend from heaven.
2. The dead in Christ shall rise first.
3. Then we which are alive and remain shall be caught up together with them.

Why? To meet the Lord. Where? In the air.

Our Lord's coming will produce a twofold effect. The righteous who will suddenly leave all their troubles behind them will have great joy. Pain, sorrow, trials, and death will be past. But terror will belong to those who do not love the Lord and are left behind.

## Accounted Worthy to Escape (Luke 21:36)

There is basic unity among evangelicals on the theme of prophecy. We agree on the fact of the Resurrection and the subjects of heaven and hell. In general, we agree that the *Bema* seat judgment for the Christians (2 Corinthians 5:10) is far removed from the judgment of the Great White Throne for the unsaved (Revelation 19:20; 20:11-15; 21:8). But there are differences of opinion with respect to the relationship of the Rapture to the Great Tribulation. Some believe in a pre-Tribulation Rapture, some in a mid-Tribulation catching away of the Church, and still others believe it will be a post-Tribulation event.

Bible students generally agree that the letters to the Thessalonians are "The Epistles of the Advent." The central passage of 1 Thessalonians is 4:13-18. The central passage of 2 Thessalonians is 2:1-12. The first passage deals with the imminent coming of Jesus as the blessed hope of the Church. The second deals with events subsequent to this.

In the first Epistle, the hearts of believers are set at rest with the assurance that they are to look for the rapture of the Church before the Millennium. The second Epistle deals with the matter of a pre-Tribulation Rapture.

In our opinion, the weight of Scripture clearly indicates a pre-Tribulation Rapture. God has "not appointed us to wrath, but to obtain salvation by our Lord Jesus, . . . that, whether we wake or sleep, we should live together with him" (1 Thessalonians 5:9, 10).

Note these reasons for believing in a pre-Tribulation Rapture:

1. The apostles were looking for the Rapture, not the Great Tribulation (1 Corinthians 15:51, 52; 1 Thessalonians 4:17; Titus 2:11-13; Philippians 4:5).

2. Jesus told us to expect Him momentarily (Matthew 24:42, 44, 50; 25:13; Luke 12:40).

3. The time of His coming is unknown (Mark 13:32).

4. This seems to be foreshadowed by the typical teaching of the Old Testament Scriptures.

5. The prophetic passages of Daniel and Revelation bear this out (Revelation 3:10).

6. Paul wrote: "Caught up together . . . to meet the Lord in the air" (1 Thessalonians 4:17). But Zechariah prophesied of the Second Coming stating: "His feet shall stand in that day upon the Mount of Olives" (Zechariah 14:4). Two events—the Rapture and the Revelation—are required to keep these passages from contradicting each other.

7. Christ will come to catch away His own and then will return "with ten thousands of his saints, to execute judgment upon all" (Jude 14, 15).

8. When the Marriage Supper of the Lamb takes place in heaven, there will be the Great Tribulation here on earth. Christ will return with His saints to put an end to the Tribulation and set up a reign of 1,000 years of peace.

The following paragraph taken from the bylaws of The General Council of the Assemblies of God states the position of our church:[3]

> The General Council of the Assemblies of God has declared itself in the Statement of Fundamental Truths that it holds to the belief in the imminent coming of the Lord as the blessed hope of the Church; and since the teaching that the Church must go through the Tribulation tends to bring confusion and division among the saints, it is recommended that all our ministers teach the imminent coming of Christ, warning all men to be prepared for that coming, which may occur at any time, and not lull their minds into complacency by any teaching that would cause them to feel that specific Tribulation events must occur before the Rapture of the saints.

### How About a Recap?

Let's have another quick look at what will happen when the Lord meets His church in the air.

*First,* there will be the resurrection of those who sleep in Jesus (1 Thessalonians 4:14). "The rest of the dead lived not again until the thousand years were finished" (Revelation 20:5).

*Second,* the living saints shall be "airlifted" and "changed in a moment" (1 Thessalonians 4:17; 1 Corinthians 15:51-57; 1 John 3:1-3).

*Third,* there will be a meeting in the air. We shall see the Lord, the One whom we having not seen yet love (John 14:1-3).

*Fourth,* there will be a great separation. Many will be left behind (Luke 17:26-36) to face the horrors of the Tribulation (Revelation 12:12).

*Fifth,* there will be the judgment seat of Christ where the saints will be judged and rewarded (1 Corinthians 3:12-15; 2 Corinthians 5:10; Romans 14:12). Our judgment as *sinners* is past (John 3:18; 5:24; Romans 8:1; 1 John 4:17). Our judgment as *sons* is present (Hebrews 12:5-11). Our judgment as *servants* will be at the judgment seat of Christ.

*Sixth,* there will be the Marriage Supper of the Lamb (Revelation 19:7-9).

## Will You Have a Nice Eternity?

The blessed hope is in a Person as well as being a:

1. *Glorious hope*—"That blessed hope, and the glorious appearing of the great God and our Saviour Jesus Christ" (Titus 2:13).

2. *Comforting hope*—"Wherefore comfort one another with these words" (1 Thessalonians 4:18).

3. *Purifying hope*—"And every man that hath this hope in him purifieth himself, even as he is pure" (1 John 3:3).

4. *Stabilizing hope*—"Be ye also patient; stablish your hearts: for the coming of the Lord draweth nigh" (James 5:8).

5. *Victorious hope*—"Then shall . . . death [be] swallowed up in victory" (1 Corinthians 15:54).

## Is the End Near?

The headlines almost scream at us that the end is near. If you're a Christian, great! If not, it's time to get ready.

Just a word, now, about your duty as a waiting Christian. You and I are to be:

1. *Watchful*—"Watch . . . for ye know not what hour" (Matthew 24:42; 25:13; 1 Thessalonians 5:6).

2. *Ready*—"Be ye also ready" (Matthew 24:44; Luke 12:35).

3. *Thoughtful*—"Gird up the loins of your mind, be sober" (1 Peter 1:13; 4:7).

4. *Faithful*—"Thou hast been faithful" (Matthew 25:21; Luke 12:42, 43; Revelation 3:10, 11).

5. *Restful*—"Ye have need of patience" (Hebrews 10:36, 37; James 5:8).

6. *Eager*—"Unto them that look for him shall he appear" (Hebrews 9:28).

7. *Holy*—"Every man that hath this hope in him purifieth himself" (1 John 3:3; 2 Peter 3:11).

---

[1] William Evans, *The Great Doctrines of the Bible* (Chicago: Moody Press, 1974 rev. ed.).

[2] Ralph W. Harris, *Our Faith and Fellowship*, Christian Faith Series (Springfield, MO: Gospel Publishing House, 1963), p. 70.

[3] General Council Bylaws, Article VIII, Doctrines and Practices Disapproved, Section 3, Eschatalogical Errors, Paragraph c., Post-Tribulation Rapture.

# 12
## *How Will It All End?*

*Read:* Revelation 19:11-15, 20; 20:1-6, 11-15; 21:1-4, 8, 23; 22:5; Isaiah 2:2-4. *Key Verse:* "Blessed and holy is he that hath part in the first resurrection" (Revelation 20:6). (See statements #14, #15, and #16 on p. 128.)

This chapter will bring to a conclusion our discussion of the doctrinal position of the Assemblies of God as outlined in the Statement of Fundamental Truths. In the preceding chapters we dealt with great doctrines that are the basis of our salvation and spiritual experiences. The last chapter was a discussion of the blessed hope.

In this chapter we wish to peer further into the future—Christ coming in His revelation, the millennial reign, the final judgment, and the new heavens and new earth.

### Now . . . Not Yet

A decade ago we were hearing about "the Pepsi generation." That generation was totally engulfed with matters that revolved around one word—*now*. Amazingly, the focus has shifted to what William Menzies terms, "Not yet."

Contemporary society is asking questions about the future. Interestingly, *Star Trek* is currently considered one of the most popular television programs. The predictions of astrologers and seers are a "bible" to multitudes.

Well, what about the future? The prophets of Scripture are preoccupied with the Lord Jesus Christ, first and last. Most often they are taken up with Christ's return to earth. One of the earliest prophecies on record concerned His return. Enoch, "the seventh from Adam," said: "The Lord cometh with ten thousands of his saints" (Jude 14, 15).

The Bible states that Jesus' feet must stand on the Mount of Olives when He returns to earth (Zechariah 14:4). He will bring His saints with Him (1 Thessalonians 3:13). World attention will focus on Him (Revelation 1:7).

At this, the second stage of His coming, He will destroy Antichrist, the man of sin, the satanic imposter who has tried to unite the world behind his master, the devil (2 Thessalonians 2:8). Satan will be bound for 1,000 years and Christ will set up His millennial reign.

But church people are divided on this matter. Is the coming of Christ premillennial or postmillennial? Or, is there a Millennium?

## What's the Millennium?

Before consideration of the above questions, we do well to define the term. The word *millennium* comes from two Latin words meaning "thousand years." Six times, in Revelation 20, we read of the kingdom lasting 1,000 years.

Presently, Christ, as the Son of God, shares the Father's throne at the right hand of the Majesty on high. He is coming to assume His own throne: "When the Son of man shall come in his glory, ... then shall he sit upon the throne of his glory" (Matthew 25:31). The Father's throne will never be shared by any creature. But Christ will

110

share His throne as the Son of Man with the over-comers (Revelation 3:21). That will be the inauguration of the Millennium.

## What Are Its Characteristics?

The Millennium will be worldwide (Isaiah 11:9; Habakkuk 2:14; Zechariah 14:9). Among animals, ferocity will give way to docility. As before the Fall, animals will be herbivorous rather than carnivorous: "The wolf also shall dwell with the lamb, and the leopard shall lie down with the kid; and the calf and the young lion and the fatling together; and a little child shall lead them. And the cow and the bear shall feed" (Isaiah 11:6-9; 65:25). The curse of the thistle, thorn, and weed will be lifted and the soil will be abundantly fertile and productive (Amos 9:13-15; Romans 8:18-23).

Wars will be banished and military equipment will be converted into implements for agriculture. Peace and harmony shall prevail. Long life will be a mark of the age (Isaiah 65:20-22). Millions will be born and these will not necessarily be regenerated when they come to the age of accountability. For this reason, when Satan is released at the end of 1,000 years (Revelation 20:7), he will be able to gather followers. But the devil and his followers will be devoured (vv. 7-10).

## Millennialism

But what about pre-, post-, and amillennialism? Here is where Christians have taken one of three positions regarding the timing of Christ's return.

*Premillennialists* hold the view that Christ will come again prior to the Millennium described in Revelation 20:4-6. In other words, Christ, coming in

111

His revelation, will usher in earth's golden age, a 1,000-year reign of peace. The government will be a theocracy (rule by God), as Christ rules over the earth. The apostles shall rule with Him (Matthew 19:28). Righteousness and justice will prevail (Isaiah 11:4). The Old Testament prophecies of Messiah's kingdom will be fulfilled.

*Postmillennialists* believe that Christ will come after the Millennium. They stake their hopes in the universal triumph of the gospel and the Church apart from the apocalyptic judgment. In their opinion, greater emphasis should be put on the requirements of the Bible that demand social justice; the elimination of such evils as war, disease, poverty, slavery, and slums; and greater stress on the efforts of all Christians to bring the Millennium about. The argument is that the Great Commission implies that the Church is to so preach the gospel as to win the whole world for Christ.

*Amillennialists* or nonmillennialists believe there will not be a Millennium. Augustine, the well-known church leader of the fifth century, moved from a premillennial to an amillennial view. He argued that there would be no future imprisonment of Satan; asserting that the devil's power had been broken when Christ died, arose, and ascended. The Church now enjoys the reign of Christ in the immediate present. Amillennialists completely spiritualize Revelation 20:4-6.

## Is Your Belief About the Millennium Important?

We recognize that premillennialism is a system of Biblical interpretation and not an essential factor in salvation. Most assuredly you can be born again and

112

not be a premillennialist. But what a man thinks about the timing of the second coming of Christ will shape his emphasis in Christian witness and service.

If you are a premillennialist—and that's where the Assemblies of God stands—you will likely be more interested in personal evangelism than in social reform. This is not because you don't believe in social reform. But the imminence of Christ's return drives you to win the lost—to put first things first.

Premillennialism brings into clear focus the responsibility of the Church to preach the gospel to the ends of the earth and to be ready for the imminent return of Christ. It recognizes the return of the Jewish remnant to the Holy Land and the reestablishment of the government of Israel. Likewise, it recognizes the refining fires of future tribulation for the nations, to be followed by Jesus' coming and the "restitution of all things" (Acts 3:20, 21).

The premillennial Christian is concerned about his present responsibilities, but he's confident about the future. He's a realist to the world situation, but he's also rejoicing in the blessed hope. He knows that: "Only one life 'twill soon be past; only what's done for Christ will last."

Concerning the Millennium, P. C. Nelson wrote:[1]

> The Lord God of heaven has decreed it; Jesus taught it; the Bible predicted it; prophets foretold it; psalmists chanted it; angels announced it; the transfiguration prefigured it; the apostles preached it; and the Cross assures it.
>
> O glorious day! for which millions of hearts have longed; for which the oppressed, the sorrowing, the suffering of the earth have cried; for which the animal creation in its suffering groans; for which all nature waits—the day of the personal, glorious reign of our Lord and Saviour Jesus Christ with His saints in robes of white and all His holy angels. O day of days for the

people of God! Then shall the children of the kingdom shine forth as the noonday sun (Matthew 13:43). The devil subdued and imprisoned, sin eliminated, sorrow past, suffering ended, tears wiped away! O glorious day! We hail thee from afar! "Even so, come, Lord Jesus" (Revelation 22:20).

## There Will Be Sinners

After the glorious reign of Christ for 1,000 years we would expect that all people would want to continue under His rule. But, though Satan will be bound, there will be people with sinful natures. Satan will then be loosed and go out to deceive the nations.

The conclusion of the Millennium will again show that if people do not choose to wholeheartedly serve Christ, they lay themselves open to satanic deception. The Bible states that after Satan is loosed, he will have an army like the sands of the sea (Revelation 20:7, 8). At this point, the Scriptures declare that "fire came down from God out of heaven, and devoured them" (v. 9). The devil will join the beast and the false prophet in the lake of fire (v. 10).

## The Great White Throne

Following the conclusion of the Millennium, there will be the judgment of the Great White Throne. The wicked dead will be resurrected to stand at the final judgment before the Great White Throne (vv. 12, 13). This will be the second resurrection. All the deeds, thoughts, and omissions will be placed alongside the standard of the Word of God to determine the degree of punishment. All will be revealed. None can hide and all will be without excuse.

# The Lake of Fire

Those whose names are not found "written in the book of life"—the subjects of this judgment—will be "cast into the lake of fire" (v. 15). Prepared for the devil and his angels (Matthew 25:41), this place we also call hell, will be the eternal abode of the wicked.

The lake of fire is described as: (1) everlasting fire (Matthew 25:41); (2) unquenchable fire (Mark 9:43); (3) black and dark (Jude 1:13); (4) constant torment with no annihilation (Revelation 14:11). Hell is also a place of extreme suffering, memory, and remorse (Luke 16:19-31), and vile companionships (Revelation 21:8).

Scripture gives a fearful picture of the punishment to which the lost will be assigned. Unlike physical death, the eternal death of the wicked has no end. The severity of eternal punishment can't be fathomed.

## Who Chooses Hell?

No one is forced to go to hell. All are urged to flee to Christ. People go to hell because they do not accept Christ (John 3:36).

In the light of coming judgment, the Great Commission places great urgency upon you and me. "Knowing therefore the terror of the Lord, we persuade men" (2 Corinthians 5:11). We need to sense this urgency as Paul did when he said: "Necessity is laid upon me; yea, woe is unto me, if I preach not the gospel!" (1 Corinthians 9:16).

## The Best to Come

The last two chapters of Revelation reveal the final issue of history. The seemingly endless struggle of all of time is past. Antichrist and the False Prophet are in the lake of fire. Satan is crushed in eternal defeat. The Resurrection is history and the judgment is ended. Our attention is now turned from the solemn descriptives of Revelation 20 to the glories of chapters 21 and 22.

The conflicts of the ages between right and wrong will be ended. The struggle between truth and error, holiness and sin, light and darkness will be over. The battle between Christ and Satan, and heaven and hell will have been won. The kingdoms of this world will become "the kingdoms of our Lord, and of his Christ" (11:15).

God's ultimate purpose is to bring heaven to earth (Deuteronomy 11:21). He purposed "that in the dispensation of the fullness of times he might gather together in one all things in Christ" (Ephesians 1:10). When that great event happens, God will "be all in all" (1 Corinthians 15:28).

## The City of the Future

"And I saw a new heaven and a new earth"—those are the cheering words of John (Revelation 21:1). And then he thrillingly states: "I . . . saw the holy city, new Jerusalem, coming down from God out of heaven, prepared as a bride adorned for her husband" (v. 2).

The picture is not of Babylon and its splendor, Athens and its intellect, or Rome and its power. Nor is it of New York and its commerce, Moscow and its force, Tokyo and its industry, or London and its greatness. From a towering mountain peak John saw "that wondrous city, the holy Jerusalem . . . filled with the glory of God," flashing and glowing "like a precious gem" (vv. 10, 11, *The Living Bible*).

## Heaven's "No Mores"

Note these thrilling descriptives of the New Jerusalem. There will be:

*No more sea.* The sea in Scripture speaks of unrest (Isaiah 57:20; Jeremiah 49:23); of mystery (Psalm 77:19); and of rebellion against God (Luke 21:25).

*No more tears.* God shall take His big handkerchief and wipe away all tears. There'll be *no crying.*

*No more death.* Life will reign. Death will be dethroned. No funeral homes or cemeteries will mar the new heaven and the new earth.

*No more sorrow.* Joy will have no shadow. No cloud will mar the landscape.

*No more pain.* No sick beds, hospitals, or suffering.

*No more sinners.* They'll all be in the lake of fire.

*No more temple.* There'll be no need of localizing worship. Every thought, every word, and every act will be "holiness unto the Lord."

*No more darkness.* There'll be no night and the Lamb will be the light.

*No more thirst.* The water of life will be freely available.

*No more sickness.* The tree of life will furnish healing.

*No more curse.* All that befell this world at the Fall will be wiped away.

A new creation—a new heaven, a new earth, and a new Jerusalem! If we are occupied with Christ and we understand the great events that are to take place and our place in the ages to come, the troubles of this life will lose their power to upset us. Our future is glorious!

---

[1] P. C. Nelson, *op. cit.*, pp. 140, 141.

# 13
## *Twentieth-century Pentecost*

The year was 1896. An itinerant lay preacher came to the home of my maternal grandparents, Mr. and Mrs. H. N. Russum, in the fertile Red River Valley at Grafton, North Dakota. My grandmother met him at the door and he inquired if he could hold a gospel service. She responded with joy for she had been converted in Minneapolis. Grandmother agreed to invite the entire neighborhood to their home.

What a remarkable meeting took place. It continued for 3 days and nights without stopping. My grandfather and many others were converted. Remarkable things occurred. One young lady, a Miss Gorder, was prostrated in a trance for hours. Suddenly she began to speak in a language that none understood.

The lay preacher listened to the girl and finally said to himself, "This must be that which was spoken by the prophet Joel." He began to search the Scriptures. Finally convinced, he sought the experience himself and received the baptism in the Holy Spirit 2 years later. That man, C. M. Hanson, became the first district superintendent of the North Central District Council of the Assemblies of God.

### Scattered Showers

The above incident is typical of numerous movings of the Holy Spirit in various places around the turn of the century. On January 1, 1901, God poured out His Spirit at the Bethel Bible College, operated by Charles F. Parham in Topeka, Kansas. Miss Agnes Ozman became the first of millions in the 20th century to receive the baptism in the Holy Spirit. It is generally agreed that it was at Topeka that the recipients, through their study of the Scriptures, came to believe that the Biblical evidence of the baptism in the Holy Spirit is speaking in other tongues.

## The Deluge Begins

The revival spread through Kansas into Missouri, Oklahoma, Arkansas, and Texas, and then leaped to California. On April 9, 1906, the Spirit began to fall on a small group of humble, hungry believers at the famous Azusa Street location in Los Angeles. Within 5 months 150 people had received the Baptism.

Listen to the description of those meetings by Ernest S. Williams, former general superintendent of the Assemblies of God. He writes:

> I wish I could describe what I saw. Prayer and worship were everywhere. The altar area was filled with seekers; some were kneeling; others were prone on the floor; some were speaking with tongues. Everyone was doing something; all seemingly were lost in God. I simply stood and looked, for I had never seen anything like it.[1]

The next month, on October 2, 1907, Brother Williams himself was filled with the Holy Spirit.

The revival spread like a prairie fire to Chicago, Winnepeg, New England, New York, Ohio, Ontario, Alaska, England, and India. T. B. Barratt of Norway received the Baptism at Azusa Street. He took the message to Norway and Sweden and a great Pentecostal work was established in Scandinavia. A similar revival broke out in a girls' orphanage in India under Pandita Ramabai.

Miss Rachel Sizelove brought the message to Springfield, Missouri from Azusa Street. Elder C. H. Mason founded the black Church of God in Christ. G. B. Cashwell carried the message to the Southeastern states. About the same time the revival broke out at the Christian and Missionary Alliance training school in Nyack, New York. Here David McDowell, Frank M. Boyd, G. F. Bender, and W. I. Evans received the Baptism, as well as others.

As with every revival, there were excesses and imperfections. Leaders began to feel the need of protecting and preserving the results. Further, speaking in tongues brought about wholesale rejection by practically every existing denomination.

## The Historic Call

A conference was called for April 2-12, 1914, at the Opera House in Hot Springs, Arkansas. Over 300 preachers and laymen came from 20 states and several foreign countries to attend this first General Council of the Assemblies of God. E. N. Bell was chairman and J. Roswell Flower served as secretary.

In calling the initial meeting, five reasons were listed for coming together at Hot Springs. These included doctrinal unity, conservation of the work, foreign missions interests, chartering churches under a common name for legal purposes, and the need for a Bible training school.

## 1916 Was Significant

The 1916 Council was crucial. The 80 delegates adopted the 16 articles in the Statement of Fundamental Truths. Because of a vital doctrinal controversy over the Godhead, as a result of the "Jesus Only" teaching, special attention was given to the section dealing with the Trinity. The Constitution and Bylaws were adopted in 1927.

In 1918 the Gospel Publishing House and the executive offices were moved to Springfield, Missouri. A $3-million four-story administration building was dedicated in 1962. A six-story international distribution center was completed in 1972.

In 1919 the Missions Department was established. That same Council adopted the *Pentecostal Evangel* as the name for its official publication. This paper was the result of a previous merger of *The Word and Witness* and *The Christian Evangel*.

## Biennial Sessions Approved

The 1921 Council made the decision to have biennial sessions. The same Council approved the establishment of a Bible school, resulting in the opening of Central Bible Institute in 1922. In 1927 the title *general superintendent* replaced *chairman* for the organization's chief officer. By action of the 1931 meeting, the Executive Presbytery was increased in number from seven to nine. The decision was made in 1935 to have each district elect two men who, together with their district superintendent, would serve on the General Presbytery.

## Significant Advances

A Home Missions and Education Department was established in 1937. They were separated in 1945. The Youth Department came into existence in 1943. A new publishing plant was approved in 1945. The national radio program *Sermons in Song* was launched in 1946. The Department of Benevolences was created in 1948. The Women's Missionary Council, now known as the Department of Women's Ministries, was launched in 1951.

In 1953, the 3-year-old *Revivaltime* radio program was placed on a national network with a full-time speaker. The Men's Department came into being in 1953. The Music Department and Church School Literature, which had been integral parts of the Gospel Publishing House for several decades, became departments in 1972. The Stewardship Department was formed the same year. In 1963, the Department of Evangelism was phased out to create the Spiritual Life–Evangelism Commission.

Evangel College, an arts-and-sciences school, was founded in 1955. The Assemblies of God Graduate School came into being in 1973. District or regionally directed schools are strategically located around the nation.

The Sunday School Department was established in 1953. Assemblies of God enrollment in 1976 was over 1.3 million, falling in fifth place nationally.

## A Milestone

Following a 4-year, in-depth, self-study, the 1971 General Council was restructured. Departments are now clustered in divisions headed by six national directors. The departments are administered by secretaries. One assistant general superintendent replaces the five previously elected. Other officers are the general superintendent, the general secretary, and the general treasurer. A 13-man Executive Presbytery serves as the church's board of directors, with a 200-man General Presbytery acting as a policy board. A congregational form of government has continued since the founding days.

The 1975 General Council saw the premiere showing of the new TV program *Turning Point* and the launching of a new home-missions thrust of establishing new churches through New Church Evangelism.

Latest statistics (1976) show the Assemblies of God has 9,140 churches, more than 20,000 credentialed ministers, over 850,000 members, and over 1.3 million adherents in the United States. Our 1,134 missionaries and 23,675 national workers serve a constituency of almost 4.6 million in 95 countries. Over 14 tons of literature pour from the presses daily to serve the needs of over 16,000 Assemblies of God and other churches in the United States.

About a life span has passed since the birth of the Pentecostal Movement. This century has seen the greatest outpouring of all time. Today the Spirit is surely falling "upon all flesh." Amazing things are happening—things that were beyond the fondest expectations of our founding fathers. People are being baptized in the Holy Spirit across denominational boundaries by the thousands.

God is moving in divine sovereignty. You can't confine God. The Spirit is like the wind which "blows where it wills." He is moving in ways that may baffle, but He is moving. Jesus promised: "I will pour out my Spirit." And He is keeping His promise!

---

[1] "Memories of Azusa Street Mission," *Pentecostal Evangel*, April 24, 1966, p. 7.

# STATEMENT OF FUNDAMENTAL TRUTHS

The Bible is our all-sufficient rule for faith and practice. This Statement of Fundamental Truths is intended simply as a basis of fellowship among us (i.e., that we all speak the same thing, 1 Cor. 1:10; Acts 2:42). The phraseology employed in this Statement is not inspired or contended for, but the truth set forth is held to be essential to a Full-Gospel ministry. No claim is made that it contains all Biblical truth, only that it covers our need as to these fundamental doctrines.

## 1. The Scriptures Inspired

The Scriptures, both the Old and New Testaments, are verbally inspired of God and are the revelation of God to man, the infallible, authoritative rule of faith and conduct (2 Tim. 3:15-17; 1 Thess. 2:13; 2 Peter 1:21).

## 2. The One True God

The one true God has revealed himself as the eternally self-existent "I AM," the Creator of heaven and earth and the Redeemer of mankind. He has further revealed himself as embodying the principles of relationship and association as Father, Son, and Holy Ghost (Deut. 6:4; Isaiah 43:10,11; Matt. 28:19; Luke 3:22).

### THE ADORABLE GODHEAD

**(a) Terms Defined**
The terms "Trinity" and "persons," as related to the Godhead, while not found in the Scriptures, are words in harmony with Scripture, whereby we may convey to others our immediate understanding of the doctrine of Christ respecting the Being of God, as distinguished from "gods many and lords many." We therefore may speak with propriety of the Lord our God, who is One Lord, as a trinity or as one Being of three persons, and still be absolutely scriptural (examples, Matt. 28:19; 2 Cor. 13:14; John 14:16,17).
**(b) Distinction and Relationship in the Godhead**
Christ taught a distinction of Persons in the Godhead which He expressed in specific terms of relationship, as Father, Son, and Holy Ghost, but that this distinction and relationship, as to its mode is inscrutable and incomprehensible, because unexplained. Luke 1:35; 1 Cor. 1:24; Matt. 11:25-27; 28:19; 2 Cor. 13:14; 1 John 1:3,4.
**(c) Unity of the One Being of Father, Son, and Holy Ghost**
Accordingly, therefore, there is that in the Son which constitutes Him the Son and not the Father; and there is that in the Holy Ghost which constitutes Him the Holy Ghost and not either the Father or the Son.

Wherefore the Father is the Begetter, the Son is the Begotten; and the Holy Ghost is the One proceeding from the Father and the Son. Therefore, because these three persons in the Godhead are in a state of unity, there is but one Lord God Almighty and His name one. John 1:18; 15:26; 17:11,21; Zech. 14:9.

**(d) Identity and Cooperation in the Godhead**

The Father, the Son, and the Holy Ghost are never identical as to Person; nor confused as to relation; nor divided in respect to the Godhead; nor opposed as to cooperation. The Son is in the Father and the Father is in the Son as to relationship. The Son is with the Father and the Father is with the Son, as to fellowship. The Father is not from the Son, but the Son is from the Father, as to authority. The Holy Ghost is from the Father and the Son proceeding, as to nature, relationship, cooperation and authority. Hence neither Person in the Godhead either exists or works separately or independently of the others. John 5:17-30,32,37; John 8:17,18.

**(e) The Title, Lord Jesus Christ**

The appellation, "Lord Jesus Christ," is a proper name. It is never applied, in the New Testament, either to the Father or to the Holy Ghost. It therefore belongs exclusively to the Son of God. Rom. 1:1-3,7; 2 John 3.

**(f) The Lord Jesus Christ, God with us**

The Lord Jesus Christ, as to His divine and eternal nature, is the proper and only Begotten of the Father, but as to His human nature, He is the proper Son of Man. He is, therefore, acknowledged to be both God and man; who because He is God and man, is "Immanuel," God with us. Matt. 1:23; 1 John 4:2,10,14; Rev. 1:13,17.

**(g) The Title, Son of God**

Since the name "Immanuel" embraces both God and man in the one Person, our Lord Jesus Christ, it follows that the title, Son of God, describes His proper deity, and the title Son of Man, His proper humanity. Therefore, the title, Son of God, belongs to the order of eternity, and the title, Son of Man to the order of time. Matt. 1:21-23; 2 John 3; 1 John 3:8; Heb. 7:3; 1:1-13.

**(h) Transgression of the Doctrine of Christ**

Wherefore, it is a transgression of the Doctrine of Christ to say that Jesus Christ derived the title, Son of God, solely from the fact of the incarnation, or because of His relation to the economy of redemption. Therefore, to deny that the Father is a real and eternal Father, and that the Son is a real and eternal Son, is a denial of the distinction and relationship in the Being of God; a denial of the Father and the Son; and a displacement of the truth that Jesus Christ is come in the flesh. 2 John 9; John 1:1,2,14,18,29,49; 1 John 2:22,23; 4:1-5; Heb. 12:2.

**(i) Exaltation of Jesus Christ as Lord**

The Son of God, our Lord Jesus Christ, having by himself purged our sins, sat down on the right hand of the Majesty on high; angels and principalities and powers having been made subject unto Him. And having been made both Lord and Christ, He sent the Holy Ghost that we, in the name of Jesus, might bow our knees and confess that Jesus Christ is Lord to the glory of God the Father until the end, when the Son shall become subject to the Father that God may be all in all. Heb. 1:3; 1 Peter 3:22; Acts 2:32-36; Rom. 14:11; 1 Cor. 15:24-28.

**(j) Equal Honor to the Father and to the Son**

Wherefore, since the Father has delivered all judgment unto the Son, it is not only the express duty of all in heaven and on earth to bow the knee, but it is an unspeakable joy in the Holy Ghost to ascribe unto the Son all the attributes of Deity, and to give Him all the honor and the glory contained in all the names and titles of the Godhead (except those which express relationship. See paragraphs b, c, and d), and thus honor the Son even as we honor the Father. John 5:22,23; 1 Peter 1:8; Rev. 5:6-14; Phil. 2:8,9; Rev. 7:9,10; 4:8-11.

## 3. The Deity of the Lord Jesus Christ

The Lord Jesus Christ is the eternal Son of God. The Scriptures declare:

(a) His virgin birth (Matthew 1:23; Luke 1:31,35).

(b) His sinless life (Hebrews 7:26; 1 Peter 2:22).

(c) His miracles (Acts 2:22; 10:38).

(d) His substitutionary work on the cross (1 Cor. 15:3; 2 Cor. 5:21).

125

(e) His bodily resurrection from the dead (Matthew 28:6; Luke 24:39; 1 Cor. 15:4).

(f) His exaltation to the right hand of God (Acts 1:9,11; 2:33; Philippians 2:9-11; Hebrews 1-3).

### 4. The Fall of Man

Man was created good and upright; for God said, "Let us make man in our image, after our likeness." However, man by voluntary transgression fell and thereby incurred not only physical death but also spiritual death, which is separation from God (Genesis 1:26,27; 2:17; 3:6; Romans 5:12-19).

### 5. The Salvation of Man

Man's only hope of redemption is through the shed blood of Jesus Christ the Son of God.

(a) Conditions to Salvation

Salvation is received through repentance toward God and faith toward the Lord Jesus Christ. By the washing of regeneration and renewing of the Holy Ghost, being justified by grace through faith, man becomes an heir of God according to the hope of eternal life (Luke 24:47; John 3:3; Romans 10:13-15; Ephesians 2:8; Titus 2:11; 3:5-7).

(b) The Evidences of Salvation

The inward evidence of salvation is the direct witness of the Spirit (Romans 8:16). The outward evidence to all men is a life of righteousness and true holiness (Eph. 4:24; Titus 2:12).

### 6. The Ordinances of the Church

(a) Baptism in Water

The ordinance of baptism by immersion is commanded in the Scriptures. All who repent and believe on Christ as Saviour and Lord are to be baptized. Thus they declare to the world that they have died with Christ and that they also have been raised with Him to walk in newness of life. (Matthew 28:19; Mark 16:16; Acts 10:47,48; Romans 6:4).

(b) Holy Communion

The Lord's Supper, consisting of the elements—bread and the fruit of the vine—is the symbol expressing our sharing the divine nature of our Lord Jesus Christ (2 Peter 1:4); a memorial of His suffering and death (1 Cor. 11:26); and a prophecy of His second coming (1 Cor. 11:26); and is enjoined on all believers "till He come!"

### 7. The Baptism in the Holy Ghost

All believers are entitled to and should ardently expect and earnestly seek the promise of the Father, the baptism in the Holy Ghost and fire, according to the command of our Lord Jesus Christ. This was the normal experience of all in the early Christian Church. With it comes the enduement of power for life and service, the bestowment of the gifts and their uses in the work of the ministry (Luke 24:49; Acts 1:4,8; 1 Cor. 12:1-31). This experience is distinct from and subsequent to the experience of the new birth (Acts 8:12-17; 10:44-46; 11:

14-16; 15:7-9). With the baptism in the Holy Ghost come such experiences as an overflowing fullness of the Spirit (John 7:37-39; Acts 4:8), a deepened reverence for God (Acts 2:43; Heb. 12:28), an intensified consecration to God and dedication to His work (Acts 2:42), and a more active love for Christ, for His Word, and for the lost (Mark 16:20).

## 8. The Evidence of the Baptism in the Holy Ghost

The baptism of believers in the Holy Ghost is witnessed by the initial physical sign of speaking with other tongues as the Spirit of God gives them utterance (Acts 2:4). The speaking in tongues in this instance is the same in essence as the gift of tongues (1 Cor. 12:4-10,28), but different in purpose and use.

## 9. Sanctification

Sanctification is an act of separation from that which is evil, and of dedication unto God (Rom. 12:1,2; 1 Thess. 5:23; Heb. 13:12). The Scriptures teach a life of "holiness without which no man shall see the Lord" (Heb. 12:14). By the power of the Holy Ghost we are able to obey the command: "Be ye holy, for I am holy" (1 Peter 1:15,16).

Sanctification is realized in the believer by recognizing his identification with Christ in His death and resurrection, and by faith reckoning daily upon the fact of that union, and by offering every faculty continually to the dominion of the Holy Spirit (Rom. 6:1-11,13; 8:1,2,13; Gal. 2:20; Phil. 2:12,13; 1 Peter 1:5).

## 10. The Church and Its Mission

The Church is the Body of Christ, the habitation of God through the Spirit, with divine appointments for the fulfillment of her great commission. Each believer, born of the Spirit, is an integral part of the General Assembly and Church of the Firstborn, which are written in heaven (Ephesians 1:22,23; 2:22; Hebrews 12:23).

Since God's purpose concerning man is to seek and to save that which is lost, to be worshiped by man, and to build a body of believers in the image of His Son, the priority reason-for-being of the Assemblies of God as part of the Church is:

a. To be an agency of God for evangelizing the world (Acts 1:8; Matthew 28:19,20; Mark 16:15,16).
b. To be a corporate body in which man may worship God (1 Corinthians 12:13).
c. To be a channel of God's purpose to build a body of saints being perfected in the image of His Son (Ephesians 4:11-16; 1 Corinthians 12:28; 1 Corinthians 14:12).

The Assemblies of God exists expressly to give continuing emphasis to this reason-for-being in the New Testament apostolic pattern by teaching and encouraging believers to be baptized in the Holy Spirit. This experience:

a. Enables them to evangelize in the power of the Spirit with accompanying supernatural signs (Mark 16:15-20; Acts 4:29-31; Hebrews 2:3,4).
b. Adds a necessary dimension to worshipful relationship with God (1 Corinthians 2:10-16; 1 Corinthians 12,13, and 14).
c. Enables them to respond to the full working of the Holy Spirit in expression of fruit and gifts and ministries as

in New Testament times for the edifying of the body of Christ (Galatians 5:22-26; 1 Corinthians 14:12; Ephesians 4:11,12; 1 Corinthians 12:28; Colossians 1:29).

## 11. The Ministry

A divinely called and scripturally ordained ministry has been provided by our Lord for the threefold purpose of leading the Church in: (1) Evangelization of the world (Mark 16:15-20), (2) Worship of God (John 4:23,24), (3) Building a body of saints being perfected in the image of His Son (Ephesians 4:11-16).

## 12. Divine Healing

Divine healing is an integral part of the gospel. Deliverance from sickness is provided for in the atonement, and is the privilege of all believers (Isaiah 53:4,5; Matt. 8:16,17; James 5:14-16).

## 13. The Blessed Hope

The resurrection of those who have fallen asleep in Christ and their translation together with those who are alive and remain unto the coming of the Lord is the imminent and blessed hope of the church (1 Thess. 4:16,17; Romans 8:23; Titus 2:13; 1 Cor. 15:51,52).

## 14. The Millennial Reign of Christ

The second coming of Christ includes the rapture of the saints, which is our blessed hope, followed by the visible return of Christ with His saints to reign on the earth for one thousand years (Zech. 14:15; Matt. 24:27,30; Revelation 1:7; 19:11-14; 20:1-6). This millennial reign will bring the salvation of national Israel (Ezekiel 37:21,22; Zephaniah 3:19,20; Romans 11:26,27) and the establishment of universal peace (Isaiah 11:6-9; Psalm 72:3-8; Micah 4:3,4).

## 15. The Final Judgment

There will be a final judgment in which the wicked dead will be raised and judged according to their works. Whosoever is not found written in the Book of Life, together with the devil and his angels, the beast and the false prophet, will be consigned to everlasting punishment in the lake which burneth with fire and brimstone, which is the second death (Matt. 25:46; Mark 9:43-48; Revelation 19:20; 20:11-15; 21:8).

## 16 The New Heavens and the New Earth

"We, according to His promise, look for new heavens and a new earth wherein dwelleth righteousness" (2 Peter 3:13; Revelation 21,22).